T0146115

Managing Public Access Microcomputers in Health Sciences Libraries

Managing Public Access Microcomputers in Health Sciences Libraries

by *Gale G. Hannigan, M.L.S., M.P.H.*
Janis F. Brown, M.L.S.

Medical Library Association, Inc.

Chicago, Illinois

MLA Information Series

This publication is printed on stock
meeting the American National
Standards, Inc. Standard Z39.48-1984
on the Permanence of Paper for Printed Library
Materials

National Library of Medicine Cataloging in Publication

Z
678.93.M53
H245m
	Hannigan, Gale G.
	    Managing public access microcomputers in
	health sciences libraries / Gale G. Hannigan,
	Janis F. Brown — Chicago, Ill. : Medical Library
	Association, c1990.
	        p.
	    ISBN 0-912176-30-X
	
	    1. Libraries, Medical. 2. Microcomputers.
	I. Title. II. Brown, Janis F.

ISBN 0-912176-30-X

To our families—Steve Bartold, and Doug, Becky, and Mandy Brown—for providing the encouragement and time necessary to write this book.

CONTENTS

FIGURES

Preface

The microcomputer is a powerful information tool that belongs among the resources of health sciences libraries. It is unique among library resources in that it is a multipurpose tool used for word processing, data analysis, education, and information retrieval and management. The computer itself accounts for only a part of its effective use; peripheral equipment, software, and people able to make them work are also necessary. The relative complexity of microcomputer resources and their multiple applications make managing microcomputers different from managing book or audiovisual collections.

Yet there are also similarities. Developing collections, providing user services, and defining appropriate staff levels are important activities in managing microcomputers, as they are in managing other library resources. Capable librarians possess information resource management skills that can make them effective managers of public access microcomputers, as well as of books and audiovisuals.

The number of microcomputers, the library's organizational context, and expectations about how the resources will be used influence management approaches and decisions. Regardless of the number of microcomputers available for public use, though, managing public access computer resources generally encompasses many activities. These include

- securing the funds necessary to purchase and maintain equipment
- planning and developing physical facilities to house and use the resources
- selecting and installing equipment, including local area networks (LANs)
- selecting and organizing software
- planning and providing services to users
- developing policies and procedures related to the use of microcomputers
- recruiting and managing staff
- promoting the resources and services

Many basic issues are the same whether the library is large or small, academic or part of a hospital. These issues include defining what level of instruction will be made available to the novice computer user, determining what type of equipment to provide, and deciding how to circulate materials. These and other issues will be addressed through suggested guidelines and by examples from different types of libraries.

This book is an effort to give practical guidance to those responsible for providing public access microcomputer resources in health sciences libraries. It is not intended for people primarily interested in automating library functions such as online public access catalogs or circulation systems.

Many products are mentioned in this book by name as examples. References to particular items are not endorsements of those products, nor should the lists of products be considered comprehensive.

Each chapter in this book focuses on a different aspect of managing microcomputer resources. Many of the activities described will, in fact, happen at the same time rather than in sequence. The chapters can be consulted independently by those readers interested in specific topics. Examples are included in the chapters.

There is a logical order to the chapters for those who choose to read the book from beginning to end. Chapter One (Incorporating Microcomputers into the Library) discusses why microcomputers belong in libraries and how they can contribute to the library's changing identity from a collection of books and journals to a focal point for information access. Chapter Two (Funding) presents a strategy for funding microcomputer resources. Chapter Three (Planning Facilities) discusses designing various work environments including individual workstations, microcomputer labs, and classrooms. Chapters Four (Equipment and Peripherals) and Five (Local Area Networks) present technical information about equipment configurations. Chapter Six (Software Collections) describes types of software and makes recommendations about purchase, installation, and organization. Chapters Seven (User Services) and Eight (Personnel) explore issues related to library support of microcomputer resources and their use. Examples illustrate what is being done in different environments. Chapter Nine (Administrative Issues) reviews the broader concerns of managers of these resources including access, fees, statistics, and cooperative arrangements.

Some topics are discussed in several chapters, each approaching the topic from a different point of view. For example, information about instructional activities appears in Chapter Three (Planning Facilities) from the perspective of planning classroom facilities, in Chapter Six (Software Collections) because of computer-assisted instruction programs, in Chapter Seven (User Services) as an example of a specialized service, and in Chapter Eight (Personnel) from the point of view of staffing to support instructional activities. The reader should find the index and chapter subheadings useful for bringing together related information.

The Appendix contains a directory of products mentioned in the text. Technical terms defined in the Glossary are italicized typically at their first occurrence.

The job of managing microcomputers is a dynamic process in a changing environment with very few traditions and rules. Our goal is to offer suggestions based on experience—ours and that of our colleagues who contributed advice and examples. Although changes in technology may quickly date this book, the underlying concepts and recommendations should be more enduring. We hope that readers will benefit from these suggestions and be better prepared to make good decisions about the management of public access microcomputer resources in their own libraries.

Acknowledgements

The authors wish to acknowledge the many individuals whose support and contributions were essential to the completion of this book. We thank the MLA Publication Panel for suggesting that we write this book, especially Dottie Eakin and Pat Walter who provided guidance in the planning stages of the manuscript, and Carolyn Weaver who was the Panel's liaison for the project. We also wish to thank the content reviewers who generously gave their time and made important comments about the manuscript. In addition, we thank the MLA Headquarters staff for their support on the project, particularly Eileen Fitzsimons, who served as coordinator and editorial consultant, Joan Grygel, project manager, and Pat Jones, our copy editor.

Our employers, Nelson Gilman, Director, Norris Medical Library, University of Southern California, and Michael M. Kitt, Vice President, International Medical Affairs, and Andrew Moriarity, Director, Medical Information, The Upjohn Company, encouraged our efforts and deserve special recognition. Staff members of Medical Library Services and the Educational Resources Division, especially Bonnie Fong, gave us much appreciated support. The Upjohn Company and the University of Southern California provided resources that made it possible for us to work together over a long distance.

This book could not have been written without the contributions of the many colleagues who shared their experiences and offered examples and advice. Among those are Shelley Bader (Himmelfarb Library, George Washington University Medical Center, Washington, DC), Laura Barrett (Library of the Health Sciences, University of Medicine and Dentistry of New Jersey, Newark, NJ), Anne Brewer (Lane Medical Library, Stanford University, Stanford, CA), Cynthia Butler (Biomedical Library, University of California, Irvine, CA), Damon Camille (Houston Academy of Medicine-Texas Medical Center Library, Houston, TX), Debra Cheney (Ellen Clarke Bertrand Library, Bucknell University, Lewisburg, PA), Stephen Clancy (Biomedical Library, University of California, Irvine, CA), Janice Contini (Louise Darling Biomedical Library, University of California, Los Angeles, CA), Virginia Cook (Health Sciences Library, Winthrop-University Hospital, Mineola, NY), James Curtis (Augustus C. Long Health Sciences Library, Columbia University, New York, NY), Shelley Davis (Greenblatt Library, Medical College of Georgia, Augusta, GA), Janet Dieman (Interactive Learning Systems, Inc., Cincinnati, OH), Judith Dowd (Medical Library, Kaiser Permanente Medical Center, Los Angeles, CA), Jacqueline Doyle (Health Science Library, Good Samaritan Medical Center, Phoenix, AZ), Carolyn Fishel

(CINAHL, Glendale, CA), Leny Freeman (Norris Medical Library, University of Southern California, Los Angeles, CA), Lelde Gilman (Louise Darling Biomedical Library, University of California, Los Angeles, CA), Vicki Glasgow (Bio-Medical Library, University of Minnesota, Minneapolis, MN), Geraldine Graves (Health Sciences Library, Kaiser Permanente Medical Center, Bellflower, CA), Susan Harker (Medical Library, VA Medical Center, Phoenix, AZ), Sherry Hartman (Schaffer Library of Health Science, Albany Medical College, Albany, NY), Beverly Hilton (Medical Center Library, University of Kentucky, Lexington, KY), Sara Hook-Shelton (Library, Indiana University School of Dentistry, Indianapolis, IN), Debra Ketchell (Health Sciences Library and Information Center, University of Washington, Seattle, WA), Paul Kittle (Medical Library & Information Center, Loma Linda University, Loma Linda, CA), Lori Klein (National Library of Medicine, Bethesda, MD), Anthony Kwak (Louise Darling Biomedical Library, University of California, Los Angeles, CA), Penny Kyker (Pitman-Moore, Inc., Terre Haute, IN), Alvin Levine (Indiana University School of Medicine, Terre Haute Center for Medical Education at Indiana State University, Terre Haute, IN), Gloria Linder (Lane Medical Library, Stanford University, Stanford, CA), Elaine Martin (Himmelfarb Health Sciences Library, George Washington University Medical Center, Washington, DC), Kenneth Martin (Norris Medical Library, University of Southern California, Los Angeles, CA), Frank Mason (Dental Library, University of Southern California, Los Angeles, CA), Lucretia McClure (Edward G. Miner Library, University of Rochester Medical Center, Rochester, NY), Marlen Paez (Stanford University Graduate School of Business Computing Facility, Stanford, CA), Chester Pletzke (Learning Resource Center, Uniformed Services University of the Health Sciences, Bethesda, MD), Lynn Povando (Himmelfarb Health Sciences Library, George Washington University Medical Center, Washington, DC), Susan Russell (Medical Center Library, University of California, Irvine, CA), Elizabeth Saltz (Fleischmann Learning Resource Center, Stanford University, Stanford, CA), Judy Sherman (Medical Library, Tarzana Medical Center, Tarzana, CA), Barbara Slater (Medical Center Library, University of California, San Diego, CA), Jocelyn TenHaken (Learning Resource Center, University of Michigan, Ann Arbor, MI), Patricia Thibodeau (Information & Media Services, Mountain Area Health Education Center, Asheville, NC), Mary Edith Walker (Medical Library, St. Jude Children's Research Hospital, Memphis, TN), Kay Wellik (Medical Library, St. Joseph's Hospital and Medical Center, Phoenix, AZ), Catherine West (University of Rochester School of Medicine and Dentistry, Rochester, NY), Margaret Wineburgh-Freed (Norris Medical Library, University of Southern California, Los Angeles, CA), Linda Suk-Ling Yau (Medical Center Library, University of California, Irvine, CA), Samir Zeind (Health Sciences Library, Huntington Memorial Hospital, Pasadena, CA).

Chapter One
Incorporating Microcomputers into the Library

This chapter provides an overview of
- the developing role of public access microcomputers in health sciences libraries
- reasons why librarians should be involved in managing public access microcomputers
- the impact of microcomputers in the library

THE ROLE OF PUBLIC ACCESS MICROCOMPUTERS IN HEALTH SCIENCES LIBRARIES

Microcomputers were first commercially available in the late 1970s. But even before the widespread availability of microcomputers, health sciences libraries acknowledged the important role of computers in supporting library user services, specifically for instruction and database searching.

Computer-Assisted Instruction

Computers were used in medical education long before the introduction of microcomputers. Results of a survey conducted in 1972 reported that 40 of 95 respondent medical schools in the United States and Canada were utilizing computer-assisted instruction to some degree.[1] Before microcomputers, computer-assisted instruction was delivered via terminals attached to large *mainframe computers. Timesharing* systems allocated a predetermined amount of computer access to the user's account. Students were given assignments to complete at the terminal; when the allocated time was spent, the student could no longer access the computer.

The introduction of microcomputers helped decentralize computing and made computers ubiquitous tools for students, faculty, and staff.[2] With microcomputers, computing became less controlled and less expensive; instructors and students could work independently of the constraints of costly mainframe computer systems and timesharing accounts. Microcomputers facilitated both the development and the delivery of computer-assisted instruction and resulted in increased use of the computer as a learning tool. Today, virtually all medical schools in the United States and Canada use computers to some extent for education,[3] and convenient access to microcomputers is expected.

Some health sciences libraries supported mainframe computing by providing a place to use computer terminals, although the operation and use of this equipment usually remained the responsibility of computer center staff. Many librarians who had provided space in their libraries for terminals also assumed responsibility for housing microcomputers. Health sciences libraries that had learning resources centers for audiovisual collections incorporated microcomputers and *software* as yet another means of delivering educational materials. Microcomputers became important educational resources that health sciences libraries were expected to have and that health sciences librarians were expected to know about.

Online Database Searching

In 1971, MEDLINE became available for librarians to search via terminals connected to the mainframe computers at the National Library of Medicine. Online database searching quickly developed into an established library service,[4] although one that, for most library users, required the expertise of a librarian intermediary with database searching skills.

The advent of microcomputers encouraged nonlibrarians to subscribe to and use online search services themselves, and online vendors began to develop "user-friendly" search systems targeted to new microcomputer users. Interest in end-user searching resulted in the placement of public access microcomputers search stations in many libraries, usually associated with reference services. The availability of *CD-ROM* versions of databases and other reference sources provided additional reasons to install microcomputers in the library.

Information Management

At a time when new information is generated at an unprecedented rate, computers enable individuals to manage—store, retrieve, manipulate, and analyze—vast amounts of data. For example, *word processing* and *file* management software make it feasible for individuals to manage large personal bibliographic files, often created through their own online searches.

Two landmark reports in the early 1980s pointed to the central role of computers in the future of information management, medical education, medical practice, and health sciences libraries. These were *Academic Information in the Academic Health Sciences Center: Roles for the Library in Information Management*[5] and *Physicians for the Twenty-First Century: Report of the Project Panel on the General Professional Education of the Physician and College Preparation for Medicine.*[6]

Academic Information in the Academic Health Sciences Center

In 1982, the *Academic Information in the Academic Health Sciences Center* report by Matheson and Cooper for the Association of American Medical Colleges articulated the vision of a future health sciences environment in which all relevant information, published and unpublished, is accessible to any person with a "need to know." In this environment, practitioners have easy access to medical literature and patient information, and researchers share unpublished data. Computers are a critical component that makes the integration of these information systems possible. This report set two important goals for the academic health sciences center:

1. The development of an academic information resources management *network* with linkages to operational information systems in the academic health sciences center and medical practice loci to facilitate the flow and use of the world's knowledge base in carrying out the functions of education, research, patient care, and management;

2. The development of academic programs that equip the faculty, the staff, and students with computational skills and information management techniques essential to effective functioning in a complex electronic information environment.[7]

Libraries are identified as a central hub for the coordination of many types of information resources and systems. The first recommendation put forth to meet these goals indicated the central role of the health sciences library:

It is recommended that institutions immediately support their health sciences libraries to strengthen their technological capabilities and develop the means to integrate the processes of academic information management with the processes of professional health education.[8]

IAIMS

In response to the report by Matheson and Cooper, the National Library of Medicine initiated, in 1983, the Integrated Academic Information Management Systems (IAIMS) program. Initially, the first awards were to support strategic planning at academic health sciences centers in creating integrated information systems; four institutions were awarded funds. Since then, the IAIMS program has provided support for projects in later phases of the development of integrated information systems, as well as related research activities. By 1990, fourteen institutions (twelve academic medical centers, one hospital, and one health professional organization) have been awarded IAIMS funds, and the term "IAIMS" evokes an important goal of many health sciences libraries.

Physicians for the Twenty-First Century

This 1984 report, commonly referred to as the GPEP (General Professional Education of the Physician) report, developed the treatise that, in medical education, learning *how* to find facts is as important as learning the facts themselves, and that the future education of medical professionals requires the development of sophisticated information skills:

Perhaps the most important concept emanating from this study is that medical students must be prepared to learn throughout their professional lives. This learning must be self-directed, active, and independent. The formal educational process should emphasize assisting the student to develop the ability and desire to continue acquiring and applying knowledge in solving problems.[9]

The computer and knowledge about how to use it were identified as elements essential for future success:

> Faculties should create opportunities for students to develop proficiency in using the computer in patient care, education, and clinical research. Medical schools should designate an academic unit charged with institutional responsibility for providing leadership in the academic application of information science and computer technology.[10]

The introduction of microcomputers, the publication of the report by Matheson and Cooper and the GPEP report, and the development of the IAIMS program pointed to change in the role of all health sciences libraries and librarians, not just those associated with medical schools. If physicians-in-training develop lifelong learning skills, including the ability to use computers, physicians-in-practice can be expected to use these skills and tools in the community. If they expect to remain an important information resource for physicians, health sciences libraries must incorporate the capability to support these information skills and tools, including microcomputers.

Library Operations

In many libraries, especially smaller ones, their first microcomputer supported library operations. Microcomputer-based file management and catalog systems brought automation to libraries that could not afford mainframe or *minicomputer* systems. *Spreadsheet* programs helped librarians organize budget information; word processing programs made producing reports and acquisitions lists much easier. *Graphics* software made it possible to design promotional materials and signs quickly and inexpensively. Often, the microcomputer and software were shared among librarians and users, creating a "semi-public" access resource.

WHY LIBRARIANS SHOULD BE INVOLVED IN THE MANAGEMENT OF PUBLIC ACCESS MICROCOMPUTERS

Computers are educational resources and tools for information access and management. Though librarians cannot claim unique responsibility for these now ubiquitous resources, there are many reasons why public access microcomputers, wherever else they are placed, also belong in libraries.
• Libraries are service-oriented organizations.
• Libraries are neutral and common territory.

- Libraries are open extended hours.
- Libraries have established systems for materials access and control.
- Libraries have a broad scope of responsibility.
- Microcomputers are integral with other library resources.
- Librarians are knowledgeable about information tools.
- Librarians have experience managing information resources.

Libraries Are Service-Oriented Organizations

Libraries are recognized, established service centers for shared access to educational and information resources. The library's primary focus is on providing service to users. Librarians are experienced in making services available to a wide range of users and are knowledgeable about developing access policies and procedures, publicizing services, and providing user assistance.

Libraries Are Neutral and Common Territory

It is easier to share resources in a neutral environment where users feel they have a right to be. For example, academic health sciences libraries that serve many different schools can provide a central facility for all students. An argument can be made to fund one shared facility that is properly supported rather than duplicate services in different schools. The same is true for a hospital library that provides services to many different user groups throughout the hospital.

Libraries Are Open Extended Hours

Libraries are often open more hours than other departments and allow access to facilities after normal, nine-to-five business hours. In many hospitals, the library is available for use by staff at all times.

Libraries Have Established Systems for Materials Access and Control

Many access and control procedures must be in place for a public facility to operate effectively. Libraries have established cataloging standards and circulation policies and procedures. They are also accustomed to providing resources while preventing loss. The risk of theft and damage is minimized, yet users can identify and use what is available.

Libraries Have a Broad Scope of Responsibility

Computer centers might be charged with providing public access facilities for word processing or similar functions; medical education departments might have facilities to support computer-assisted instruction. The library's mission can be broad enough to encompass these and other education- and information-related activities. Some organizations have microcomputer resources—hardware and software—but do little to provide educational support for the user. Libraries can be places where people not only have access to resources but get support in learning how to use them.

Microcomputers Are Integral with Other Library Resources

Increasingly, information and instruction are being delivered via computer technologies. While the "electronic book" has not replaced traditional hardcopy collections, standard medical library service now includes access to information in electronic formats. Interactive *videodisc*, online search services, and CD-ROM collections are all examples of the growing presence of computer-based educational and information resources in libraries. If libraries are to continue as a primary source of information and instructional materials, it is essential that libraries continue to incorporate computer technologies and support their use.

Librarians Are Knowledgeable about Information Tools

Librarians bring significant expertise to computer-related issues and activities. For example, database creation is a popular microcomputer application. As experienced managers of large collections and catalogs, librarians understand the concepts of developing and maintaining text databases. As expert searchers of online bibliographic and full-text databases, librarians know the characteristics of successful retrieval systems.

Librarians Have Experience Managing Information Resources

Librarians have a long tradition of information management expertise that they can translate from book and journal collections to electronic information collections. Many organizations are getting involved in IAIMS-type projects. Knowledgeable librarians can address issues related to the integration of text databases and the availability of commercial databases. Librarians can also contribute valuable insight about the anticipated use of information retrieval systems and the types of user services needed to support them. The microcomputer is a key tool in the future development and management of information resources.

THE IMPACT OF MICROCOMPUTERS IN THE LIBRARY

Introducing public access microcomputers into the library results in a significantly different level of demand for local support and involvement compared to print and audiovisual collections. Microcomputers and their use are different enough from other library materials that their addition can significantly affect the role and identity of the library itself. The following are some of the issues that will be addressed in more detail within specific chapters of this book.

The Resource

Microcomputer resources are varied and complex. Equipment malfunctions; programs give cryptic error messages. Optimal hardware configurations change rapidly. IBM PC centers become IBM PS/2-dominated, and later include Macintosh equipment, as the result of large grants or institutional agreements. The media librarian's tradition of choosing a format and standardizing on it does not apply to microcomputer resources simply because the technology continually changes.

Software is different from books and audiovisual materials such as videocassette and slide/tape programs. Software is available on disks or distributed through networks. Programs can be recreational, educational, or both, broadening the scope of how computers are used and creating a demand for on-site software collections. Software can be modified either by design or by mistake. Sometimes it must be modified to work on the available equipment. Not all software works on all computers. The amount of computer memory and the type of coprocessor and graphics display are important considerations in software purchase and use. Licensing arrangements are more complex, expensive, and uncertain than those established for most audiovisual programs.

Use

People who never used the library before come to use the microcomputers. People who have never used a computer come to the library to learn how. These new and novice users need assistance beyond the level of instruction previously provided in libraries. Other users are expert and teach librarians about the equipment and software. Problems associated with operating microcomputers are local and immediate rather than in the domain of staff from a large, remote computer system. Thus, the person responsible for the place where microcomputers are located becomes, especially from the user's point of view, responsible for microcomputer operation and use.

Many librarians find that the library's identification as a center for computing activity and expertise changes the library's image from a repository of books and journals to an exciting place to be, where people can experiment with new information technologies. Issues beyond the basics of microcomputer operations arise. These involve access, security, collections, and circulation policy.

Organizational Role and Identity

Public access microcomputers were placed in many libraries to make a costly resource available to many users. The degree of external interest, participation, and sometimes control, in developing and determining how microcomputers are used in libraries has been significant, perhaps more than with any other library resource. This level of involvement can be both threatening and exciting; it can change the relationship between librarians and users, affecting the autonomous and sometimes isolated role of the library within the parent organization. It may juxtapose the library's role in contrast to the roles of other information organizations, such as the computer center, and raise issues about the library's unique value and purpose.

This juxtaposition is highlighted by the issue of who controls the microcomputer resources. The equipment may be purchased by a department or computer center and placed in the library for easy access by the most users. Questions arise regarding: Who has the expertise to manage the resource and assist the users; who will arrange and pay for maintenance and equipment upgrades; who will set policies and take responsibility for the future development of the resource? These issues are discussed in the context of Funding (Chapter Two) and Administrative Issues (Chapter Nine).

SUMMARY

Microcomputers are essential tools for health sciences education and information access and management. Like other important information tools, they belong in health sciences libraries. The complexity and versatility of microcomputers and microcomputer use result in a greater demand on library staff. The development and management of public access microcomputer resources in the library presents new challenges to the librarian and may affect the role of the library itself.

References

1. Brigham CR, Kamp M. The current status of computer-assisted instruction in the health sciences. J Med Educ 1974 Mar;49(3):278–9.
2. Van Houweling DE. The information network: its structure and role in higher education. Library Hi Tech 1987 Summer;5(2):7–17.
3. Piemme TE. Computer-assisted learning and evaluation in medicine. JAMA 1988 Jul 15;260(3):367–72.
4. Darling L, ed. Handbook of medical library practice. 4th ed. vol. 1: public services in health science libraries. Chicago: Medical Library Association, 1982, 157–8.
5. Matheson NW, Cooper JAD. Academic information in the academic health sciences center. Roles for the library in information management. J Med Educ 1982 Oct;57(10 pt 2):1–93.
6. Physicians for the twenty-first century. Report of the Project Panel on the General Professional Education of the Physician and College Preparation for Medicine. J Med Educ 1984 Nov;59(11 pt 2):1–208.
7. Matheson NW, Cooper JAD. Academic information in the academic health sciences center. Roles for the library in information management. J Med Educ 1982 Oct;57(10 pt 2):74.
8. Matheson NW, Cooper JAD. Academic information in the academic health sciences center. Roles for the library in information management. J Med Educ 1982 Oct;57(10 pt 2):74.
9. Physicians for the twenty-first century. Report of the Project Panel on the General Professional Education of the Physician and College Preparation for Medicine. J Med Educ 1984 Nov;59(11 pt 2):29–30.
10. Physicians for the twenty-first century. Report of the Project Panel on the General Professional Education of the Physician and College Preparation for Medicine. J Med Educ 1984 Nov;59(11 pt 2):128.

Further Reading

Broering NC, ed. Symposium on integrated academic information management systems. Bull Med Libr Assoc 1986 Jul;74(3):234–61.

Matheson NW, ed. Symposium: Integrated academic information management systems (IAIMS) model development. Bull Med Libr Assoc 1988 Jul;76(3):221–67.

Chapter Two

Funding

This chapter reviews activities related to funding public access microcomputer resources, including
- defining objectives
- specifying what is needed to accomplish those objectives
- identifying funding sources
- developing a funding proposal
- getting support for the proposal
- dealing with partial funding, gifts, and cooperative arrangements

The goal of this chapter is to suggest a strategy for getting resources support. Specific information about facilities planning can be found in Chapter Three (Planning Facilities); Chapter Four (Equipment and *Peripherals*) discusses equipment purchase decisions and budgets; Chapter Eight (Personnel) reviews staffing needs.

DEFINING OBJECTIVES

Microcomputer use is now widespread and cannot be claimed exclusively by any single discipline. This often results in intense competition for microcomputer resources among individual departments in an organization, including the library.

Funding requests from the library, whose broad mission is to support the information and educational activities of its clientele, may not fare well when considered alongside a clinical laboratory's specific need for automated tracking systems equipment or a faculty request for computer equipment to augment grant-related or publication activities. The computer center's administration may claim a central role in supporting educational computing as an extension of its support of other computing activities. Even within the library, public access microcomputer resources may be of secondary importance compared to the need for equipment to support administrative or library systems automation activities. Particularly in times of fiscal constraint, it is necessary to compete with other important projects for limited resources.

Competing successfully for support typically requires persuading those who allocate funds that the outcome envisioned deserves, or even demands, implementation. Especially in seeking funds for new technologies, it is easy to fall into the trap of focusing on things rather than results. If everybody wants a microcomputer (a thing), then the request must focus on the results of obtaining the microcomputer: how it will be used to benefit the organization or help meet the objectives of the funding source. More critical than deciding what equipment to buy or what staff it will require is developing, communicating, and selling a concept of how public access microcomputer resources will contribute significantly to the library's important role in the organization.

To do this, it is helpful to take the following steps:

1. Relate the need for microcomputers to the library's mission.
2. Define the library's organizational context as it relates to public access microcomputers.
3. Specify the objective: what will be achieved.

Relate the Need for Microcomputers to the Library's Mission

First, review the library's mission to ascertain how adding public access microcomputers can support it.

For example, a large academic health sciences library includes a learning resources center whose mission is to support the instructional and self-instructional activities of health sciences students and faculty. The increasing role of computer-assisted learning in health sciences education requires that computer equipment and software be available to students and faculty in the library.

Another example is the hospital library charged with providing current, accurate information resources to meet the patient-care information needs of its clinical staff. The availability of online and CD-ROM reference sources and databases enhances the individual staff member's access to current information and supports the mission of the library.

Define the Library's Organizational Context as It Relates to Public Access Microcomputers

Next, address the questions, What unique or critical contribution can the library make with regard to microcomputer access? and Why is the library the best place to locate these resources? To answer these questions, one needs to know about the parent organization, its mission, and its facilities, as well as the services offered by other departments. The library may be in competition with other departments for finite computer resources; unjustified duplication of resources is usually discouraged. Turf battles over which department controls which service can be destructive and a waste of time and energy. Focus on the positive contributions the library can make. The issue here is What does the library have to offer that is unique and of benefit to the organization as a whole?

For instance, make the point that the library already has in place the overhead structure, services, and staff needed to provide access to resources such as microcomputers. Locating microcomputers in the library may result in significant cost savings compared to the expense of developing a microcomputer facility elsewhere.

As another example, use the fact that many organizations are adopting an IAIMS-type approach to their information resources. This approach promotes a central role for the library in the integration of information. The library (an existing educational service center) and librarians (experts in resource management and teaching users about information resources) have a legitimate role in the organization's efforts to develop public access to electronic information systems.

Other, general reasons why public access microcomputers belong in health sciences libraries are discussed in Chapter One (Incorporating Microcomputers into the Library). Some of them may be appropriate to include in your argument.

Don't forget to review the possible arguments that other departments or individuals seeking support may make. Criteria such as cost, expertise, space, access to and distribution of resources, and staffing are important considerations for judging competing proposals. How well you can anticipate this information in other proposals provides a perspective on how your proposal may fare and also enables you to incorporate points that highlight the comparative strength of your argument.

Defining the library's organizational context as it relates to public access computers can reveal how the library may fit into the organization's information plan, as well as predict possible success in obtaining funds.

Example from a Funding Proposal

What follows is an excerpt from the "Background" section of a funding proposal that reviews the library's mission as it relates to microcomputers, defines the library's organizational context, specifies the objective of having microcomputers in the library, and generally lays the groundwork for the request for funding.

Example

The Indiana University School of Dentistry Library is considered one of the largest dental libraries in the United States. Its 25,000 books and 650 current subscriptions support the teaching, research, and service mission of the School of Dentistry. In addition, an effort is made to make the Library's materials available to dental health professionals throughout the country and to the citizens of Indiana.

The Library staff is small, but provides a wide variety of services, from ordering and cataloging books and journals, to interlibrary loan, research assistance, and computerized literature searching. Throughout the years, new technologies have been implemented in all areas of library activities. For example, a new system (CD-ROM) was recently added to help students and faculty gain access to journal articles in a manner which may be less expensive than traditional online systems. Similarly, Computer Education and Training is another indication of the Library's attempts to integrate technology into the teaching and research functions of the School of Dentistry.

Computer Education and Training was introduced to the Indiana University School of Dentistry in May, 1986. Designed to promote greater *computer literacy* among faculty, staff, and students at the School of Dentistry, the program was implemented with two IBM Personal Computers and a wide variety of software packages, manuals, tutorials, and videotape programs. . . . At the time, no one could have predicted the popularity of such a program, or the resulting demand for additional equipment. Even the purchase of a third computer has proven inadequate to serve a student population of 500 and 150 faculty members.

The primary objective of Computer Education and Training is to provide faculty, staff, and students at Indiana University School of Dentistry with the opportunity to use computers. Many of the students will graduate and take positions in offices where computers are used for patient records, billing, and general correspondence. Some of the students graduating from the dental curriculum may even purchase computers for their own offices. To choose among the dozens of available systems is confusing; a poor decision can be costly. It was hoped that exposure to computers and a wide variety of software packages now would prepare students, as well as faculty and staff, for selecting and using computers throughout their professional careers.

Secondly, Computer Education and Training was developed to help faculty, staff, and students at the School of Dentistry manage their work here at the School of Dentistry more efficiently. Many individuals find these computers invaluable tools for completing assignments, typing research and patient reports, and for learning about ledgers and budgeting. Computer Education and Training has been particularly beneficial to graduate students, who must prepare an extensive thesis prior to completing their programs. Similarly, class notetakers have found that the use of computers greatly simplifies the process of generating scripts of weekly lectures for distribution to classmates.

(Indiana University School of Dentistry Library, used with permission)

Specify What Is to Be Achieved

Addressing the library's mission and organizational context should help clarify what you intend to achieve. You will have the background information to answer the most important question: *Why* should *this* library get the requested support? Among the specific objectives often cited are

- to provide shared access to equipment that is in demand or very expensive
- to provide access to library resources such as online catalogs and bibliographic databases
- to link library users with mainframe systems or external databases including clinical information systems
- to encourage the development of computer applications in education and research
- to promote computer literacy
- to support the curriculum of the institution
- to provide a central facility for formal group instruction
- to provide a demonstration site for people interested in evaluating microcomputer equipment and software.

Examples from Funding Requests
The following are examples of objectives taken from requests for funding microcomputer resources.

Example
Request for Funds to Support Microcomputer Consulting
If funded, the following services would then be provided:
1. Microcomputer network management and support including equipment troubleshooting.
2. Scheduled and "on demand" consulting services for health science students and faculty requiring personalized assistance with microcomputers and software.
3. Short courses for faculty, staff, and students regarding the use of specific health sciences software.
4. Coordination/facilitation of microcomputer "interest" groups in the health sciences.

(University of Minnesota Bio-Medical Library, used with permission)

Example
Request for Funds to Develop a Local Area Network
The project's five specific aims are to:
1. Develop information-seeking skills for first- and second-year medical students by providing unlimited access to a multi-type CD-ROM network, to include MEDLINE, a scientific reference tool, and word processing.
2. Link student computer *workstations* to the ISU automated library system to enhance local access to materials.
3. Enhance access to other materials by facsimile transmission of articles.
4. Provide instruction in computer literacy skills.

5. Provide a central hardware resource with sufficient capacity for expansion to support the addition of computer assisted instruction and wet lab simulations.

(Indiana University Medical School, Terre Haute Center for Medical Education at Indiana State University, used with permission)

SPECIFYING WHAT IS NEEDED

Early in the planning process, it is necessary to identify what kinds of resources will be needed to meet the proposed objective. One goal of this book is to help librarians define the various components associated with providing public access microcomputer resources. The book's chapter headings can serve as a prompt for the categories of resources (equipment, personnel, etc.) that should be reviewed. Some chapters have checklists and worksheets that can be used to specify items and costs. It is useful to consult with colleagues who are involved in similar projects and ask questions such as, What would you do differently the next time? and What unexpected needs came up? If possible, visit microcomputer facilities in other libraries to see what works well and why.

You should plan to spend time investigating software requirements, equipment capabilities, furniture configurations, layouts, and licensing agreements. Don't forget to account for depreciation, replacement, maintenance, and repair in your plans and budget. Some of this groundwork can be delegated, but make sure that you still have a good understanding of what is planned. Know what you need and why you need it so that you are prepared to defend or modify the request if necessary. Get second opinions and explanations; get estimates and proposals in writing. See things in operation, including equipment configured as you want it and software performing as expected. Be wary about "planned upgrades" and offers to customize equipment or software to your specifications. Don't pay in advance for these promises, and do make contingency plans in case they are not fulfilled.

Example
                Specifications for a Local Area Network
The proposed local area network must be able to:
   – handle 70 *nodes*
   – handle 30 simultaneous users with reasonable response time
   – handle more than 100 software programs and provide 150 *MB* of storage for software and files
   – handle IBM *DOS*
   – *interface* with the university's *telecommunication* system
   – provide shared *modem* and printer access
   – call into and out of the *LAN*

– provide various security and usage levels
– provide *electronic mail.*

(University of Southern California Norris Medical Library, used with permission)

IDENTIFYING FUNDING SOURCES

Professional organizations, vendors, government and private agencies, social groups, and individuals are all potential sources of funds. A list of selected funding resources appears at the end of this chapter. Before approaching a funding agency, investigate the guidelines of your own organization and do some background research on potential funding sources.

Institutional Guidelines

There seems to be a trend toward more coordinated purchasing and reliance on institutional discount arrangements with vendors. Librarians must consider the direction of technology development within their parent organization when planning to seek support for microcomputer resources. Legal and fiscal requirements may prohibit an individual, at any administrative level, from entering into an agreement to purchase computer technology without going through a formal institutional review process.

The first step, then, is to check with your parent institution to find out about

- institutional policies and procedures regarding solicitation of funds
- established sources of funding within the organization
- discount agreements with equipment and software vendors
- local funding resources that might support your specific objectives, for example, a medical education fund

Finding Out about Funding Sources

Make sure the library is on all appropriate mailing lists used to distribute announcements of funding opportunities. Librarians, especially those not considered part of the faculty or the administration, can be overlooked when mailings are sent regarding grants and other funding sources. If the library cannot get on these lists, ask faculty or administrator friends of the library to pass these announcements on to you.

Funding can come from within the institution, from affiliated organizations, or from other grant-awarding organizations. Promoting awareness of the library's need for funds can result in funding information or support as the following examples illustrate.

Example
A dental school library solicited funds from the school's alumni organization to purchase microcomputers. The school's graduating class presented the library with a *desktop* publishing system.

Example

One academic medical center library received most of its budget for equipment from annual donations by a hospital volunteers group. Although these donations were not guaranteed, yearly proposals have resulted in annual gifts.

Example

A two-year medical school program solicited and received a grant from the U.S. Public Health Service to develop microcomputer resources. The funding agency had announced, in the *Federal Register*, a request for funding proposals that was limited to two-year medical schools. A university development officer saw the announcement and passed it on to the dean of the medical school.

Example

A library in a teaching hospital experiencing budget cuts developed proposals and then received funding from the medical staff association and individual physicians. Over a three-year period, they funded two microcomputers with printers and a MEDLINE CD-ROM system.

Agencies and programs usually have criteria to determine whether or not a request is appropriate. It is useful to ask targeted agencies for their funding guidelines and for information about recently funded projects. Take the time to determine how well your proposal meets these restrictions and fits these criteria before spending time putting together a customized package for a particular agency.

DEVELOPING A FUNDING PROPOSAL

Funding requests should be carefully planned but flexible. They should take into account local restrictions and resources, such as organizational support of particular vendors through institutional discount programs. Some of the sources for information about funding proposals are listed at the end of this chapter. This section focuses on the major components of typical proposals and includes examples relevant to microcomputer-related requests.

Statement of Purpose

Though individual institutions and funding resources have preferred formats for funding requests, it is uniformly essential, in both planning and seeking funding, to be clear about objectives. The approach likely to be successful incorporates concise statements of

- what is wanted
- why it is being requested
- what objective benefit will accrue, and to whom, if the proposed plan is implemented

Example

Request for Additional Microcomputers

Five more public access microcomputers are needed in the library to meet the increased demand for access. Currently, an average of three people are waiting to use microcomputers at any given time. Five additional workstations should alleviate this wait, as well as provide for expected increased demand in the short-term future.

Example

Request for Letter Quality Printers

At least one letter quality printer is needed in the library so that microcomputer users can produce final copies of their work on-site. At this time, users typically leave the library to go to an off-campus print shop and pay $1.00 per page for letter quality output. If the library met this need, users would save time. Charging for the service could recover operating costs.

Example

Request for Upgrade of Existing Equipment

The most current versions of software used in this institution cannot be used on the library's computers at this time. Upgrading the memory capability on each computer from 640K to 2MB will make it possible to use what are now the standard versions of these programs.

You will, of course, need additional explanation and justification. But it is useful to state clearly the "what and why" of your proposal early on. Senior level administrators and committees responsible for funding decisions appreciate an easily identifiable, succinct statement of purpose.

Documenting Support

When seeking resources for any service, don't overlook the valuable support of current and potential users. Obtain evidence of user needs and interests by
- collecting use statistics
- recording user suggestions
- soliciting comments about how the proposed service might be used

A request that addresses the expressed needs of many users might be looked upon favorably as a reasonable way to satisfy people across the organization, as illustrated by the examples below.

Example

A physiology faculty member wants students to use an instructional videodisc program. His department is interested, but cannot fund the equipment purchase. His written request leads the library to seek funding for an interactive videodisc workstation that would be available both to students in the physiology class and for other educational programs.

Example

A hospital's administration is interested in providing alternative ways for its medical staff to acquire continuing medical education credit. The library suggests developing a collection of computer-assisted instruction programs that offer continuing education credit for physicians, as well as provide training opportunities, and perhaps credit, for other professional staff.

Example

Users of an academic health sciences library want access from the library's microcomputers to other university information resources including a locally mounted MEDLINE database and various clinical information systems. A local area network would provide the easiest and most cost-effective method of accomplishing this, as well as improve the distribution of other software programs.

The Specifics

At some point in the proposal you must provide exact information about what you want and the resources needed (money, staff, and effort) to get it. This is the place for equipment specifications, facilities layouts, furniture descriptions, staffing requirements, and the estimated cost for each item. Other chapters in this book discuss these specifications in detail.

Unless the proposal is to a particular funding source, such as a computer vendor, or a specific brand of equipment is needed, it is best not to limit the request to a particular brand or model. This is because

- funding sources may want to determine the brand, eliminating from competition those proposals specifying other brands
- the funding source or parent organization may insist on choosing suppliers based on competitive bids
- the technology and price may change from the time the request is made to when the funds become available

To maintain flexibility, use phrases that indicate equivalence or *compatibility*, for example, "IBM PS/2 with 2MB of memory or equivalent computer" or "*laser printer* compatible with WordPerfect." Of course, if there are compelling reasons to specify a brand, do so and give the reasons why. In any case, state in writing that final approval of what to buy rests with you, not with a purchasing agent or committee. The particular brand purchased may determine the furniture required (not all *IBM PC compatibles* are the same size, for example) and affect maintenance agreements and ease of use (as with different keyboards in a classroom). You are the person to determine equivalence or compatibility; the proposal should state this.

GETTING SUPPORT FOR THE PROPOSAL

Getting support for your proposal involves translating the objective into a realistic, specific, and desirable vision of the future and campaigning on its behalf.

From a librarian's point of view, public access microcomputers logically belong in libraries. This notion may not be obvious to a hospital administrator, the head of a computer center, or a faculty researcher who makes funding decisions or is in competition with the library for funds. Unfortunately, as much effort as goes into selling the concept of microcomputers in libraries may also have to go into selling the concept of the library as an important player in the organization's overall plan for managing information resources.

The traditional image of "library work" needs revision to encompass all of the sophisticated information management and access systems now used in most health sciences libraries. What librarians now take for granted in terms of text information and retrieval systems is the goal of many administrators with data processing experience. It may help your case to point to the many ways modern medical libraries employ computers to handle everyday activities and how much integration of library information resources has already been achieved by online catalogs and circulation systems.

Inform library users about efforts to get funds. Let them know that the library is actively pursuing new or improved services. Awareness of the library's goals may also engender support if its users participate in funding decisions or have discussions with people who do.

Proving that the library can provide access to resources more economically is a persuasive argument, but underestimating cost in order to be competitive is a dangerous strategy when results are judged. Be realistic and don't overlook the hidden costs of increased demand on existing staff and facilities. Although the price tag is a critical discriminating factor among proposals, perceived benefit to the goals of the parent organization often carries more weight than simple economy. The concept or scenario that meshes with other goals of the organization is more likely to be supported, even if it is more expensive.

PARTIAL FUNDING, GIFTS, AND COOPERATIVE ARRANGEMENTS

The ideal is to get enough unrestricted money from one place to match your request. However, it is common that one agency will fund equipment only, while another source will support renovation or staffing, for example. Even if you approach one source for all components, you need to plan a strategy for handling partial funding.

Only you can make a realistic assessment of what resources are essential to meet your objectives. Settling for less may guarantee failure; refusing to accept less can jeopardize the opportunity for any involvement at all. Good judgment and good negotiation skills are critical here. It may be possible to modify plans without changing objectives. Your request may be for 25 computers and a local area network to support computer literacy. Funding may be for five computers, no network. You can still support computer literacy, but not to the same degree and probably not as planned; it will be necessary to modify expectations. Funding for equipment but not for furniture is a dilemma, and its resolution depends on whether or not you can make the equipment usable. Functional access to the microcomputers is more important than how they are housed. Accepting equipment without support for repairs, maintenance, and upgrade is risky because it establishes a level of service that may not be maintained over time.

Sometimes it is appropriate to decline offers to support the development of microcomputer resources. Undesirable gifts include outdated or cast-off equipment, software that requires nonstandard equipment configuration, and equipment meant for only a select user population. Each of these situations requires individual consideration and judgment, but library administrators have the right and responsibility to refuse anything that impedes the library's mission by diverting resources or discriminating against users.

Competitors for funding are also potential allies in a cooperative proposal. Since the expense of computer resources can be significant, organizations may look favorably on requests that satisfy more than one expressed need. Another reason to look to your colleagues is that cooperative arrangements can "stretch" the dollar and result in even better outcomes for the library and its users.

Reports of the success of cooperative efforts vary. A common situation is placing microcomputers in the library, but leaving administration to the computer center. This arrangement takes advantage of the library's hours of access and typically central location. What the library gets in return is identification with and easy access to new technology. Whether or not the arrangement works depends on how well expectations are defined and met and on the quality of contingency plans and communication when circumstances change.

Cooperative arrangements raise important and interesting issues. Chapter Nine (Administrative Issues) includes a discussion of cooperative efforts.

SUMMARY

Efforts to get funding for microcomputer resources can be more competitive and creative than seeking funds for many other library services. Developing a funding proposal is an opportunity to define the library's role in the organization as it relates to the use of microcomputers. Funding proposals must specify what is needed and why; funding arrangements must be consistent with the overall objectives of the library.

Funding Sources

MLA Research, Development, and Demonstration Project Grants
   Medical Library Association
   Six North Michigan Avenue, Suite 300
   Chicago, IL 60602

National Library of Medicine
   Extramural Programs
   National Library of Medicine
   Building 38A, Room 5S-520
   Bethesda, MD 20894

Institutional groups such as alumni, auxiliary, friends, volunteers

Institutional funds such as educational fund, bequests

Computer companies (contact regional sales representatives)

Guides

Courses, workshops, and presentations offered at professional meetings
   such as the Health Sciences Communications Association, the Medical
   Library Association, the Special Libraries Association, and the
   American Library Association

Books, guides, and reports available from
The Foundation Center
   79 Fifth Avenue, Dept. EC
   New York, NY 10003

Guides and advice from the Regional Medical Library Program (RML);
for the address of your region's RML contact
National Library of Medicine
   Building 38A, Room 5S-520
   Bethesda, MD 20894

McClure CR, et al. Planning and role setting for public libraries: a
   manual of options and procedures. Chicago: American Library
   Association, 1987.

Chapter Three
Planning Facilities

This chapter covers planning microcomputer facilities, including
- deciding where to locate microcomputers in the library
- configuring microcomputer work environments for specific types of use
- estimating the cost of establishing different types of work environments

Chapter Four (Equipment and Peripherals) focuses on the equipment itself. The goal of this chapter is to review the characteristics of microcomputer work environments for individual and group use, including
- the single-user workstation
- multi-workstation microcomputer labs
- microcomputer classrooms

LOCATING MICROCOMPUTERS IN THE LIBRARY

Where to locate a single-user microcomputer workstation, a microcomputer lab, or a microcomputer classroom within the library is best determined by taking into account each of these factors:
- space availability
- electrical availability
- accessibility by staff
- noise containment
- visibility
- security

Space Availability

Space availability is usually the primary deciding factor in locating microcomputers because space is often at a premium in libraries. In a one-room hospital library, space is probably the only factor to consider. It helps to be creative and to consider all usable space; sometimes available space can be identified by rethinking the current allocation of space. See figure 3.1.

Example

In one academic medical library, space for end-user workstations was created in the reference area by discarding some little-used reference materials and shifting other materials to eliminate the need for two index tables.

Example

   In the medical library of a small hospital, the librarian solved the space problem in her 400-square-foot library by putting two microcomputer workstations on carts. Each microcomputer could be moved to wherever it was needed and moved away from prime space when not in use.

Example

   In a medium-sized teaching hospital library, one librarian made efficient use of available space by housing a microcomputer, a videocassette player, and their shared *monitor* in each media carrel.

Electrical Availability

   Availability of electrical sources also is a primary factor in deciding location of microcomputer facilities. Library space may not have an abundant supply of electrical outlets. Adding equipment that requires electricity may also mean bringing electricity to the equipment. Consultation with the institution's building engineer or electrician is necessary if modifications to the building electrical system are being considered. Some buildings can accommodate changes to electrical wiring; other buildings may be less flexible.

   Extension cords and multioutlet electrical strips are alternate ways to bring electricity to the equipment. Electricians may need to be consulted to determine the electrical load on a circuit. Adding microcomputer workstations to the same electrical circuit used for other office equipment can result in power supply problems. Consistent power without brownouts or surges is important to avoid damage to the equipment and the data stored on microcomputers. For user safety, electrical cords should not be stretched across traffic areas. Cable runners to cover electrical cords may reduce the possibility of a user tripping, but will not eliminate it.

Example

   A dental school library wanting four microcomputer workstations for public use was faced with the dilemma of having all the wall space occupied by shelving and of being unable to use under-the-floor or behind-the-wall solutions to supply electricity. The solution was to cluster the workstations together and run extension cords to them from the closest outlets and across the shortest expanse and least used traffic area. Cable runners over the cords have so far prevented users (or staff) from tripping.

Example

   A medium-sized academic medical library wanting to establish microcomputer workstations throughout the library resorted to different solutions for different areas. For workstations in a center island, electricians installed new electrical outlets in the floor by running wires

Figure 3.1. Floor Plan of Microcomputers Integrated throughout a Library

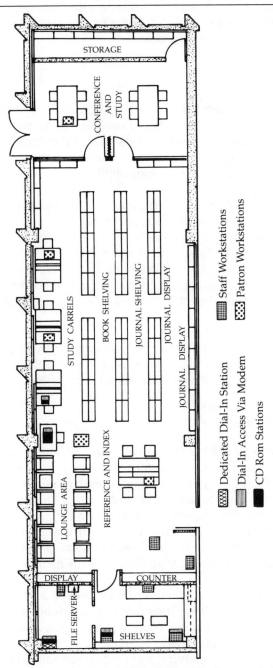

(Loma Linda University Medical Center, Medical Library & Information Center, used with permission)

under the flooring. For workstations located against a wall, extension cords provided a simple solution with no safety problem for users.

If alternative sites are available, or if a new facility is being planned, other factors are important to consider.

Accessibility

A key factor is the accessibility of the microcomputers to library staff working in other service areas. Microcomputer users require assistance. Proximity of the microcomputer workstations to the library service staff is essential to provide quick assistance to users and to minimize the time library staff is away from other responsibilities such as covering a service desk.

The optimal location of microcomputers within the library depends on who is responsible for providing support services. For example, end-user searching stations are best placed in reference areas for easy access to reference librarians. See figure 3.2. If a user needs to borrow items at the library's circulation desk, the workstations should be close to that service area. Although it is not an optimal situation, a microcomputer shared by library staff and users should be placed as conveniently as possible for both.

Classrooms are best situated near the library's entrance or should have a separate entrance to minimize disruption caused by large groups entering and leaving. Instructors often require access to telephones and support staff, therefore easy access to service points is important, too.

Noise Containment

Noise containment is a very important issue in determining the location of public access microcomputers. Microcomputer facilities are not quiet areas: keyboard keys click; dot-matrix printers are notoriously noisy; and conversations take place between staff and users or among the users themselves. Microcomputers should be located away from quiet study areas. Areas that are already noisy, such as the reference area, or where users are buffered from outside noise by earphones and carrels, such as the media center, can be good locations for public access microcomputers. See figure 3.3.

Larger microcomputer facilities should be housed in a defined and isolated part of the library. Group instruction is best done in a separate classroom designed for that purpose. When it is not possible to have a separate classroom, acoustic partitions may help create a contained environment. At the very least, a way of reserving a cluster of workstations for group instruction should be determined and obvious to other users who are working on their own. See figure 3.4.

Figure 3.2. Floor Plan Showing Proximity of End-User Searching Stations
to the Reference Desk

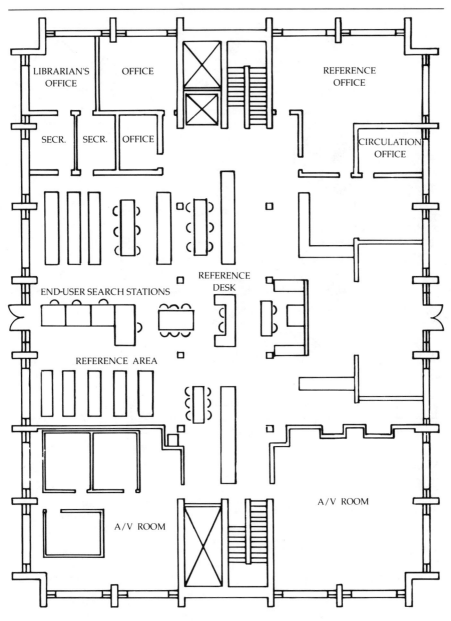

Figure 3.3. Floor Plan of a Combined Media and Microcomputer Area

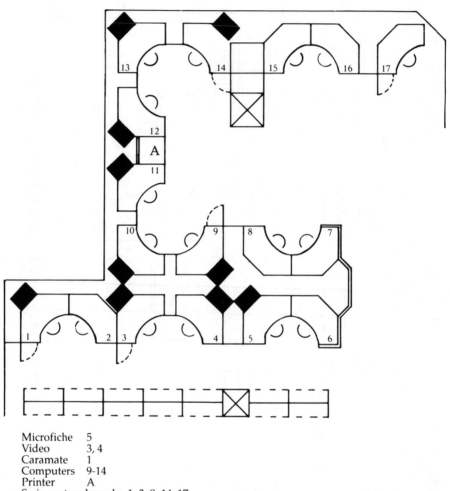

Microfiche   5
Video   3, 4
Caramate   1
Computers   9-14
Printer   A
Swingout endpanels 1, 3, 9, 14, 17

Visibility

Visibility is another factor in determining where to locate microcomputers in the library. Users expect to find books and journals in the library and will ask for them if they are not visible. Microcomputers are not as directly

Figure 3.4. Floor Plan of a Library Microcomputer Facility with a Separate Classroom

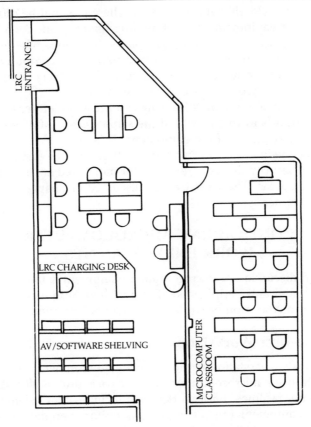

(University of California, Irvine, Medical Center Library, used with permission)

associated with libraries; they should be either easily visible to users or advertised. When microcomputers have high visibility, they promote the resource and emphasize the library's participation in the use of computer technology. Users who may not read signs directing them to the micro-computer facility or may not pick up fliers describing the library's micro-computer resources will notice a microcomputer in a high-traffic area.

One academic medical library first placed an interactive video worksta-tion near the library's entrance, then moved the workstation to its perma-nent location in a less visible area once users were aware of the new library service.

Security

Security is another factor in deciding where to locate microcomputers. They can be placed in a locked room, with access restricted to authorized users. This arrangement is not optimal since security is compromised as soon as one user is given access to the room. An alternative is to locate workstations in a closely supervised area where it would be difficult for a user to remove equipment without alerting library staff. As a minimum precaution, microcomputers should be placed in an area where there is at least the illusion of monitoring by library staff. Microcomputers in areas remote from staff are more susceptible to theft. Portable computers and computers on carts require a secure storage area.

An academic health sciences learning resources center kept four microcomputers on carts in rooms behind the service desk. After hours, someone stole various pieces of the equipment. This event led to securing the equipment in media carrels in an open area that could be easily monitored.

Additional security devices are useful for monitored areas and essential for less secure areas. These devices are discussed in Chapter Four (Equipment and Peripherals).

CONFIGURING MICROCOMPUTER WORK ENVIRONMENTS

A detailed discussion of microcomputer equipment is found in Chapter Four (Equipment and Peripherals). The goal here is to focus on the configuration of microcomputer work environments for various kinds of use.

The Single-User Workstation

A single-user workstation is the complete environment required by an individual to use a microcomputer. It is the basic unit of all public access microcomputer facilities. Each workstation includes these elements:
- computer equipment (microcomputer, monitor, peripherals such as a printer)
- furniture (work surface, chair)
- power supply

Computer Equipment

As with any electronic equipment, microcomputers have environmental requirements, which are usually noted in the equipment manual under "system requirements" or "equipment specifications." The average air-conditioned library typically meets these requirements. Most microcomputers require temperatures between 50 degrees F and 104 degrees F in order to operate reliably. Microcomputers do need to be kept away from very dusty areas and extremes in temperatures.

Glare from sunlight or diffused overhead fluorescent lighting reflected on monitors can make reading a monitor's screen difficult. Use of color monitors, especially, can be hindered by glare. Indirect or *parabolic lighting*, antiglare screens, or simply aligning the monitor in a different direction from the light source may alleviate the problem of glare. Tilt and swivel stands for monitors help in adjusting them away from glare. Curtains or blinds for windows are another solution.

A workstation also might include many pieces of peripheral equipment such as printers, modems, videodisc players, CD-ROM drives, *optical scanners, mouse* devices, etc. Peripheral equipment can consume a large portion of the work space.

Though ease of use is a major factor in designing an appropriate work environment for peripheral equipment, it must be balanced with the need to provide adequate user work space. Printers should be close enough for users to examine and retrieve *printouts,* but their location should not usurp prime user work space. Before deciding where to place a printer, consider the following: access to the printer for loading paper; a place to stack printer output; space for storing paper at the workstation; and acoustic hoods to reduce printer noise. Laser printers and other large printers usually require a separate stand or table.

CD-ROM drives and videodisc players can be placed toward the outer boundaries of the work space since they usually require user involvement only at the beginning and end of a session. If theft is a problem, small peripheral pieces that cannot be easily secured and are not high-use items can be provided as needed instead of left at the workstation. For example, a mouse for an IBM PC or a 5.25" external *disk drive* for a Macintosh might be made available only on request.

If the workstation is portable, on a cart, for example, then all individual elements should be securely attached. The use of multiple-outlet power strips can reduce the amount of effort involved in moving the workstation with all its various components.

Furniture

Furnishings for microcomputer work environments need not be elaborate. But certain features in the furnishings can make the work environment more comfortable and more functional.

The microcomputer work surface may be a standard library table or desk or a specially designed microcomputer table, carrel, or cart. There are many design options to consider.

Carrels provide privacy for the user, minimize distractions, and are especially useful when workstations are arranged next to or across from one another. Many users prefer a private and defined work area. However, when partitions are more than 51 inches high, they may hamper the ability of library staff to monitor computer use.

Microcomputer tables are typically less expensive than carrels. The openness of microcomputer tables may make some users feel more exposed and less comfortable. On the other hand, the use of tables can foster interaction between users, encouraging people to seek help from each other. Some microcomputer tables incorporate security units as part of the furniture design.

The type of microcomputer to be used is an essential consideration in choosing furniture. A Macintosh SE, a Macintosh II, an IBM PS/2 Model 50, and an IBM PS/2 Model 80 each differs in shape and size. As a result, each has its own space requirements.

The height of the keyboard work surface should be approximately 26 inches, the same as is recommended for typing stands. This is especially important for the users' comfort over long periods of "keyboarding" for word processing or other applications. Some microcomputer tables provide special adjustable keyboard sections. These tables often have 28.5-inch-high work surfaces, which are more comfortable for writing and are especially useful for classroom workstations where users may spend as much time writing as keyboarding. Keyboard trays can be purchased separately and attached to standard desks or tables. In all cases, make sure that the tray is easy to adjust and sturdy. Sometimes an adjustable chair can meet the same need.

Wheelchair access is another consideration in determining table heights. At least one work surface should be 28–30 inches high to accommodate users in wheelchairs.

A user requires an area at least 20 inches by 16 inches for writing notes, spreading out paperwork, using manuals, etc. Users also need space for personal belongings such as purses and backpacks. Some microcomputer tables provide shelving under the table to store belongings or to stack peripherals; make sure these do not interfere with leg room. Computer supply catalogs and stores sell stands for setting the microcomputer on its side underneath the work surface and support arms for holding monitors above, thus clearing the work surface for the user. Some furniture is designed with shelving for component parts. In any case, try to provide the largest work surface possible.

Different furniture may be needed for different types of equipment configurations. Examine alternatives before making the decision to purchase. A table may be suitable for a microcomputer, but an interactive video station with two monitors, a microcomputer, and a videodisc player may fit more compactly into a carrel designed to hold them. See figure 3.5. An end-user workstation with a local CD-ROM unit, a printer, and space for manuals and search tools requires considerably more space than a workstation used for standard computer-assisted instruction. The dimensions for the CD-ROM work surface should be approximately 60 inches by 30 inches. The dimensions for a basic instructional workstation, without peripherals, can be smaller, approximately 42 inches by 30 inches.

Library architectural standards recommend that the minimum work surface for a microcomputer-based workstation should be 10 square feet (48 inches by 30 inches) with an additional 19 square feet of circulating space, raising the minimum space requirement per person to 30 square feet.[1]

Flexibility is a key design factor. Furniture that is custom made for a specific computer may be useless when that computer is replaced by an-

Figure 3.5. Sample Interactive Video Carrel

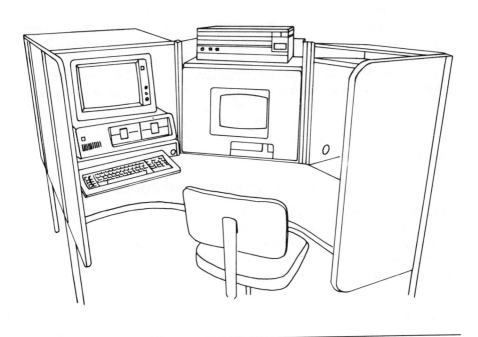

other model. Microcomputer furniture is available from a variety of sources including library and computer supply catalogs, library and media furniture manufacturers, as well as furniture stores.

Existing library furniture can be used if it meets the basic requirements for microcomputer use. To determine if the work surface dimensions are adequate, measure the total dimensions of the microcomputer including the keyboard. If the space is enclosed, as in a carrel or against the wall, the measurements should include room for the cables that are connected to the back of the microcomputer. An IBM PS/2 Model 50 requires a work surface 28 inches deep; a Macintosh SE requires a work surface 20 inches deep. Typing stands and carrels can accommodate microcomputers by attaching keyboard trays that pull out from underneath the work surface. The height of the work surface can be adjusted by cutting off 2.5 inches from the legs of a standard 28.5-inch-high table.

The chair is another element of the workstation. The chair should be similar to those provided in library office areas rather than those in the reading and study areas of the library. It must be easily adjusted to accommodate different users. The "ideal" chair rolls or slides, swivels, has a padded seat and back, and is adjustable for seat height and for chair back angle. Arms on the chair are desirable but not essential. Many libraries cut costs by economizing on chairs. However, users are not comfortable sitting on straight-backed chairs with hard plastic seats and backs.

Power Supply

Depending on the number of peripherals, multiple-outlet power strips may be needed. Surge-protected outlets are essential. These can be a built-in feature of the workstation furniture or the security system, or they can be purchased separately. The electrical cords and cables connecting peripheral equipment to the microcomputer can create a tangled mass of wires. Coiling and binding excess lengths, or using cable channels available from computer supply catalogs and stores, can help control cables. Outlets and cables should be out of the user's way to avoid inadvertent unplugging of wires.

Multi-Workstation Microcomputer Laboratories

For purposes of discussion, any cluster of microcomputer workstations configured primarily for individual use is considered a microcomputer laboratory. Since the individual workstation is the basic component of a lab, the previous Single-User Workstation section is relevant to planning microcomputer labs, too. Emphasis here is on the characteristics of larger microcomputer laboratories—those with five or more workstations.

Service Areas

On-site staff support is recommended for user consultation in microcomputer laboratories and is discussed in Chapter Eight (Personnel). Staff need a defined location, with a table or desk, where users can get assistance. A microcomputer for the consultant is not essential since users most frequently need assistance at their own workstations. However, access to a microcomputer allows the consultant to perform other computer-related activities in between requests for help. A telephone gives the consultant easy access to other resources such as computer center help-lines and reference services. Providing a modem or some other access to computer-based resources also is helpful for a consultant trying to locate information or test systems. If consultant assistance is not provided whenever the facility is open, then a telephone and numbers to call for assistance provide a minimal level of service. The area may need shelving and a service counter if it also serves as the circulation point for the microcomputer software collection.

Users should have easy access to reference sources such as equipment manuals, software manuals, dictionaries (both medical and English), and brief guides to the software collection or to the use of the equipment. A bulletin board is useful for posting announcements, general information, and helpful hints. A *white board* is good for providing rapidly changing information, such as user queues and the consultant's hours or current availability. See figure 3.6.

Figure 3.6. A Microcomputer Laboratory Layout

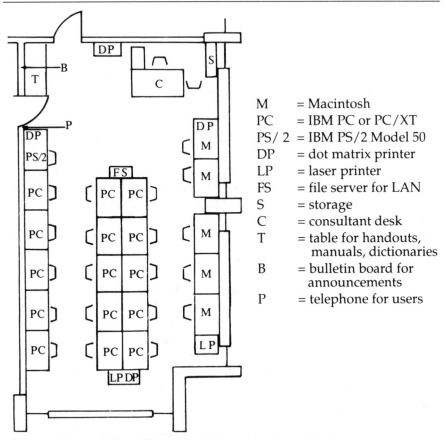

M   = Macintosh
PC   = IBM PC or PC/XT
PS/ 2 = IBM PS/2 Model 50
DP   = dot matrix printer
LP   = laser printer
FS   = file server for LAN
S   = storage
C   = consultant desk
T   = table for handouts,
             manuals, dictionaries
B   = bulletin board for
             announcements
P   = telephone for users

(University of Southern California, Norris Medical Library, used with permission)

Shelving and Storage

Shelving needs depend on the size and use of the software collection and related materials. If the software collection circulates, shelving will be needed to organize and house it. If the software is distributed to users through a local area network, as described in Chapter Five (Local Area Networks), less shelving is needed. However, some shelving still will be required to store software that cannot be readily or legally installed on a network and software manuals. File cabinets can be used for storing software, but they may not be practical for storing bulky manuals.

Supplies such as printer ribbons, laser printer toner *cartridges*, ink cartridges, disks, cleaning materials, and printer paper should be stored within or near the user area. The storage space should be a lockable cabinet or file drawers. If large quantities of supplies are used, additional storage space will be necessary.

A larger secure storage area away from users can be used for

- large quantities of printer paper for replenishing supplies kept in the user area
- multiple copies of software when additional copies are required by license agreement or copyright
- spare parts such as disk drives, *circuit boards,* cables, and even spare microcomputers, monitors, and modems for replacing defective equipment

It also is a good idea to have a secure work area away from user space for

- receiving and storing equipment until it can be made available to users
- setting up new equipment, installing circuit boards, making repairs
- housing local area network administrative equipment including central *file servers, asynchronous* communications servers, CD-ROM network servers, *uninterruptible power supplies,* and other equipment that should be protected; note that the location of this equipment may be determined by network specifications

Shared Printers

When just a few microcomputers are available for public use, they are usually established as complete *stand-alone* workstations. However, in a larger microcomputer laboratory the workstations may share peripherals.

Users can get easily confused if shared equipment is not logically located. A printer shared by two workstations should be placed between them. A printer shared by more than two microcomputers warrants its own table and ought to be adjacent to the workstations it serves—at the end of a row, for example.

Some libraries charge for the use of printers. Depending upon the charging system, printers may need to be located behind a service desk or in a separate room where they can be monitoried or the service mediated if necessary.

Layout

Planning for the microcomputer laboratory itself is similar to any library space planning effort. Suggested readings are included at the end of this chapter.

Ease of use is one of the main considerations in arranging the workstations in the laboratory. Sufficient aisle space, at least 20 inches, allows users and library staff to move freely between the workstations without disrupting other people. Wheelchairs require 44 inches for aisle space and even more for turning space, so some workstations should be in more open areas for easier access.

If more than one type of computer equipment configuration is available, grouping similar workstation configurations together helps a user quickly identify the equipment desired. See figure 3.7. For example, a laboratory

Figure 3.7. Floor Plan Showing Clustering of Similar Types of Microcomputers

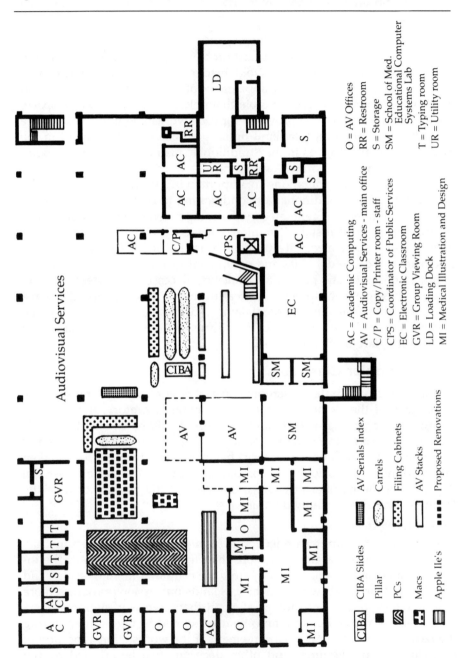

(Medical College of Georgia, Robert B. Greenblatt, M.D. Library, Audiovisual Services, used with permission)

might have one cluster of IBM PS/2 Model 55sx microcomputers with color monitors and another cluster with Macintosh SE/30s and IIci's grouped together.

Environment

Cable control becomes a significant problem when there are several microcomputer workstations. To avoid inadvertent user interference with cables, as well as to enhance the appearance of the lab, cables can be routed under table tops and encased in cable channels. In renovated or new space, electrical outlets should be provided for each workstation; this will reduce cable chaos, although it may limit options for changing the layout in the future. Raised flooring, as in the "traditional" mainframe computer room, provides another solution for cable control.

Environmental considerations are important in a microcomputer lab. The facility may require additional air conditioning to compensate for the increased amount of heat generated by the equipment and users in the space. If carpeting is to be installed, minimize static electricity by selecting carpeting with a static electricity propensity rating of 2.0 *KV* or less. Static electricity can cause data loss and equipment malfunction. The KV rating indicates the antistatic protection available. Recessed incandescent spotlights reduce glare; however, that feature needs to be balanced against increased heat from incandescent lamps. Baffles for fluorescent lights, which direct the light down rather than diffuse it throughout the room, can also reduce glare on the monitors.

Microcomputer Classrooms

Since a microcomputer classroom consists of workstations and incorporates many of the elements of a microcomputer laboratory, the previous information regarding workstations and labs should be taken into consideration. The classroom, whether dedicated to group instruction or used as a combination classroom/laboratory, has additional features to be taken into account. The feasibility of combining a laboratory and a classroom depends on the number of courses offered and the amount of time the facility is available for individual use.

Projection Systems

Some type of computer projection system greatly enhances an instructor's ability to teach a group of more than five students. With it, the instructor can display images directly from the computer monitor screen and use the software itself while teaching. Hands-on sessions progress more quickly when students can follow along at their own workstations.

The type of projection system to be used should be determined during the facilities planning stage. Arrangement of the workstations, location of projector screens, lighting, and other decisions will be affected by the projection system used.

A variety of projection systems are available including video projectors, *LCD* video projectors, data display systems that work with overhead projectors, and television-type large screen monitors. Each has its own requirements. Video projectors provide the largest, sharpest images, approximately 6 feet by 8 feet. Television-type monitors provide the smallest images, although 40-inch diagonal monitors are now available. Further details about this equipment are provided in Chapter Four (Equipment and Peripherals).

Video projectors must be set at a fixed distance from the projection screen. Video projectors permanently mounted on the ceiling do not take up classroom space and do not require refocusing and adjustment after initial set-up. If the projector is portable, space for it must be provided and readjustments made each time it is moved. The manufacturer's specifications should indicate how far to place the projector from the screen for a specified projected image size. These specifications should be carefully considered in determining the location of the projector. For a ceiling-mounted projector, existing conduits or other building features may interfere with placement.

LCD video projectors and data display systems that work with overhead projectors must be at some distance from the screen to give a large, focused image. The overhead projector itself can obstruct the students' view of the screen, so its placement should be carefully considered when designing the classroom.

Both video projectors and data displays require projection screens. A wall-mounted screen, especially for large screens, provides a flatter surface for a more focused image. Different types of screens are available, for example, *lenticular,* matte white, or glass beaded. Screen selection should be based upon the room dimensions, room lighting, and projector image brightness.

Monitors do not require the strict lighting conditions that projection systems do. However, they do need to be carefully situated to allow students to see the images easily. For large-screen television-type monitors, one is needed for every group of five to seven students. In a local area network environment, ordinary computer monitors can be used to display images from the instructor's station. Since these monitors are small, at least one is needed for every two students in addition to the monitor at each student's workstation. See figure 3.8.

Local area network software, like PC Chalkboard, makes it possible to display images from one monitor to many monitors, such as from the instructor's workstation to the students' workstations. This allows each student to see the demonstration, but does not permit the student to work along with the instructor.

Cables for the projector or monitor should be kept away from the aisles. For a ceiling-mounted video projector, the cables connecting it to the in-

Figure 3.8. Floor Plan of a Networked Classroom Using Shared Monitors

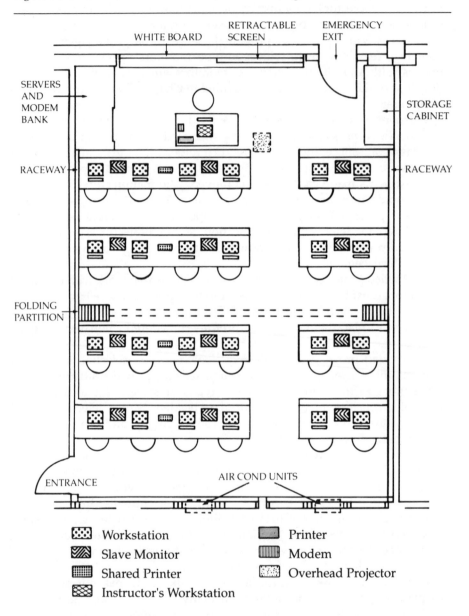

(Stanford University, Lane Medical Library, Medical Informatics Technology Laboratory, used with permission)

structor's station should run above the ceiling and through the walls. Electrical outlets also are required for these projection devices. For a ceiling-mounted video projector, add an outlet in the ceiling.

Instructor's Workstation

The instructor's workstation requires more space than a typical workstation in order to accommodate teaching materials and additional equipment. It also may need to accommodate equipment brought in for special sessions, such as CD-ROM drives, modems, and other peripherals. Instructors may prefer to stand at the workstation for easier movement to the white board, projection screen, or other equipment. A higher workstation is desirable. (See figure 3.9.) Some computer furniture is designed espe-

Figure 3.9. Example of a Stand-up Workstation for Instructors

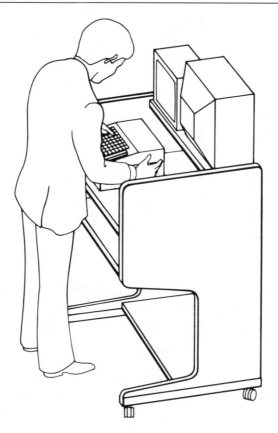

(Synsor Corporation, used with permission)

Figure 3.10. Floor Plan of a *U*-Shaped Microcomputer Classroom

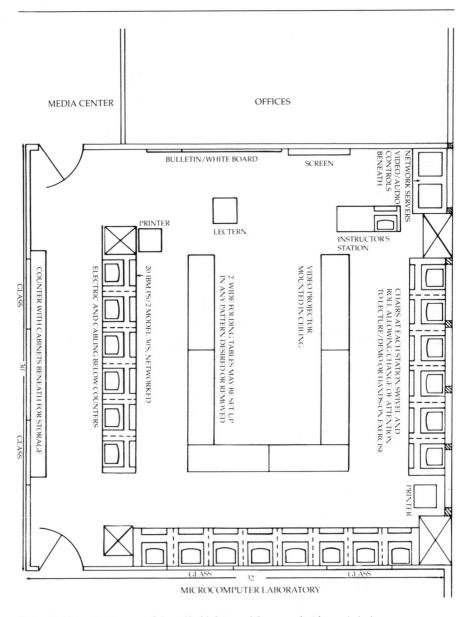

(Columbia University, Augustus C. Long Health Sciences Library, used with permission)

cially for presentations using an LCD display with an overhead projector. Although they do not provide much space beyond that required for the microcomputer and overhead projector, they may be a useful configuration.

The location of the instructor's workstation may depend upon the projection system and its cables. Cable length may limit the distance between the instructor's workstation and the projection system. When cables can be extended and routed away from the user area, then placement of the instructor station is more flexible. Neither the instructor nor the workstation should block the students' view of the projection screen.

The monitors at student workstations also can block the view between the students and the instructor. To avoid this

- set the monitor to one side of the student workstation
- provide an indentation in the student workstation that lowers the monitor
- arrange the student workstations in a U-shape with the instructor's station at the top of the U and the students sitting on the inside of the U (See figure 3.10.)
- raise the instructor area on a platform or stage so that the instructor and students can see one another

The last option is effective, but requires providing safety precautions against instructors tripping on the steps to the platform, especially in a darkened room. Footlights and/or handrails on the steps should be installed.

Other Teaching Aids

Other useful items in a classroom include a white board and audiovisual equipment. White boards are recommended over chalk boards because they generate less dust. An overhead projector and a slide projector are useful teaching aids often requested by instructors. Short focal-length lenses can be purchased that allow slide projectors to produce a large image when placed only a short distance from the projection screen. A projection booth in the rear of the classroom is another option. An extra table, or shelving, is useful for handouts and other teaching materials. A bulletin board for the classroom can be used for posting classroom announcements, schedules, etc.

A clip-on microphone system makes it easier for students to hear over the ambient sound of microcomputers and reduces stress on the instructor.

Layout

A microcomputer facility used for group instruction should be arranged like a classroom, with the instructor's workstation facing the student workstations and the students oriented toward the instructor. As with the microcomputer laboratory, adequate space is required for working at the microcomputer and for walking around students who are seated. The instructor must be able to reach all of the students in the classroom, not just those who are at the end of a row.

Having the same type of computer equipment at the instructor's workstation and all student workstations minimizes confusion and facilitates instruction. Even the difference between color and *monochrome* monitors can cause confusion. It is best if the instructor can give one set of instructions to all students, rather than different instructions for students at different equipment configurations.

There are practical limits to the number of workstations in a classroom. One instructor can effectively monitor about 20 workstations, fewer if the students are very inexperienced or the class content is very complex.

Lighting

Proper lighting in the classroom is essential when projection systems are used. Students need sufficient lighting at each workstation to see the keyboard and to take notes. They also need to see the white board and projected images. However, the projection screen must be kept dark for a clear image.

Recessed incandescent downlights are recommended. Downlights scatter light over the student and instructor workstations and do not interfere with the projected image the way fluorescent lighting does. Fluorescent lighting can be used if the light is directed down and not diffused throughout the room.

Lights that can be dimmed or turned off in part of the room allow the lighting to be adjusted to an appropriate level. Light switches should be located near the instructor, who can make adjustments easily without having to ask for assistance. Lighting in the classroom must be separate from other library lighting so that the instructor can control the room lighting without affecting other work areas.

ESTIMATING COSTS

Figure 3.11 is a guide to determining the costs associated with purchasing a single-user workstation and developing a microcomputer laboratory or classroom. Amounts are given to provide a general idea of costs involved. They reflect costs in 1989, but will fluctuate greatly if different equipment brands and models are purchased. Ongoing costs, for supplies, telephone service, etc., are not included.

Figure 3.11 Sample One-Time Costs

Workstation

IBM PS/2 Model 55sx with 60MB hard disk	$3,200
Macintosh SE/30 with 40MB hard disk	3,500
dot-matrix printer	450
laser printer	4,500
modem (2400 *baud*)	440
4 drive CD-ROM unit	3,500
interactive video carrel	1,300
chair	180
table	185
security devices	$30–$250

Microcomputer Laboratory*

cabinet (72″ high)	$175
shelving (6 shelves)	200
table (30″ × 60″)	330
bulletin board (fabric covered)	60
printer table	110
phone installation	75
consultant's desk	500

Microcomputer Classroom*

instructor station	$360
LCD display	1,800
overhead projector	390
overhead projector cart	276
video projector	11,000
projector screen (6′ × 8′)	385
white board (96″ × 48″)	135
table (18″ × 30″)	100
slide projector	460
slide projector cart	200
short focal length lens	65

*Combine with costs for workstations.

SUMMARY

This chapter has described microcomputer facilities in general. A particular library must develop its own microcomputer facility with the money and space available. If the library can provide only a donated microcomputer on a table that is too high and narrow, with a hard, straight-back plastic chair that does not swivel or roll, then so be it. The user at least has access to a microcomputer. There may be complaints and probably frustration, but the less-than-ideal, heavily used workstation may also provide an incentive to advocate for better or additional workstations.

Reference

1. Information technology and space planning. Library Systems Newsletter 1985 Nov;5(11): 83.

Additional Resources

Gaylord Furniture Layout Kit
    Gaylord Bros., Inc.
    P.O. Box 4901
    Syracuse, NY 13221
    (800) 448-6150; (315) 457-5070 in New York State

Gaylord Microcomputer Layout Kit
    Gaylord Bros., Inc.
    P.O. Box 4901
    Syracuse, NY 13221
    (800) 448-6150; (315) 457-5070 in New York State

Further Reading

Cohen A, Cohen E. Designing and space planning for libraries: a behavioral guide. New York: Bowker, 1979.

Leighton PD, Weber DC. Planning academic and research library buildings. Chicago: American Library Association, 1986.

Pulgram WL, Stonis RE. Designing the automated office: a guide for architects, interior designers, space planners, and facility managers. New York: Whitney Library of Design, 1984.

Chapter Four
Equipment and Peripherals

This chapter covers aspects of microcomputer equipment and peripherals, such as printers and videodisc players, including
- purchase and replacement
- installation
- preventive maintenance and repair

Our recommendations are intended to provide some general guidelines for making decisions. We do not recommend purchase of specific equipment since institutional considerations should prevail and because any such recommendations become quickly outdated.

This chapter does not cover everything needed to make the equipment available for public use. Furniture and other environmental features are discussed in Chapter Three (Planning Facilities). Due to the complexity and extent of the subject, information about local area networks is discussed separately in Chapter Five (Local Area Networks).

"Everything-you-need-to-know" about microcomputer equipment is a topic worthy of many books, rather than just one chapter. Additional readings for more in-depth coverage of microcomputers are listed at the end of the chapter. Although much of the information provided applies to a variety of situations, when appropriate, the focus is on factors of concern to health sciences librarians.

PURCHASING AND REPLACING EQUIPMENT

When purchasing equipment, libraries should follow some general guidelines.

Hardware Decisions Are Software Driven

The first rule is to purchase equipment compatible with the software that will be used. This applies to the microcomputer and all the peripherals. Don't be swayed by high-pressured sales talk into buying the most expensive models that will "do everything." Also don't be coerced into taking some other department's outdated equipment. Have a good idea of the software that will be provided, and investigate its equipment requirements. Does the software work on a Macintosh only, and does that Macintosh need to be a IIci with a color monitor? Is the software compatible with the printer or CD-ROM drive you want to buy? Recommendations from colleagues who are providing the types of software and services that you are planning may be helpful.

Go Along with the Crowd

Librarians should stay in the mainstream when purchasing microcomputer equipment. Buying "standard" equipment means that there will be

- fewer software incompatibility problems and a greater variety of available software
- more local sources for technical advice, maintenance, and repairs, usually resulting in lower costs for such support
- more options for add-ons such as circuit boards, peripherals
- fewer problems connecting to other systems within the institution
- more users who are already familiar with the equipment

A health sciences library is likely to collect a variety of software including programs developed at the institution or at other health sciences schools. The availability of standard equipment encourages the development of programs that can be exchanged between institutions.

Don't Be a Trailblazer

Seek the best of the current technology, but be careful of being the first to acquire the latest innovation. If the equipment can use existing software as well as open up new possibilities for the future, then it is a good candidate for purchase.

Allegiance Is Not Always a Virtue

Buying the same equipment in quantity can be advantageous. Volume discounts may be available when large quantities are purchased. Maintenance and repair may be less expensive since contracts can be consolidated and service calls can be coordinated. As equipment gets older, one unit can be *"cannibalized"* for replacement parts for other units. It is easier to provide user support, such as instructions and guides, when many people are using the same kind of equipment.

However, allegiance to one *operating system* limits opportunities to use software that is only available for another operating system. Some educational software for health sciences curricula is available for only Macintosh or only IBM-compatible environments; providing only one type of equipment eliminates use of some high quality software. Also, getting the best price in the current market may be more difficult if one is not willing to consider other brands.

You Get What You Pay For—Usually

Although no other microcomputers are compatible with the Macintosh, there are a multitude of choices among other types of equipment, such as IBM-compatible microcomputers and printers. Price is a major determining factor in deciding which type of equipment to purchase; however, it should not be the only factor. Paying extra for reputation, research and development, corporate overhead, and user support may be worthwhile when problems arise. Buying a well-known brand of equipment also provides some security for its future longevity. When the library needs a replacement part three years later, the manufacturer will most likely still be in business and support the product. This does not imply that one should buy only from Apple or IBM. There are many other manufacturers selling quality products, a few of which are Compaq, Hewlett-Packard, AST Research, and Epson. Mail-order products and local brands may also be good investments if adequate technical support and repair services are available.

The Job Is Never Done

No matter how well one tries to anticipate the future, there will be new enhancements to equipment and changes in technology. Microcomputer equipment purchase is not a one-time, never-again effort. Three to five years of use may be the longest that can be expected. On the other hand, it is not wise to hold off purchase while waiting for the next big development. Try to weigh the value of currently available, proven products against the usefulness of what you already have. A major change should be prompted by significant improvements; otherwise, it may make more sense simply to upgrade existing equipment. Regardless of when the equipment is purchased, a new development will soon occur.

Basic Buying Tips

To help decide *what* to buy, read reviews. The following computer journals are a few of many that include equipment reviews:

Byte—for all microcomputers
InfoWorld—for all microcomputers
MacUser—for Macintosh computers
MacWorld—for Macintosh computers
PC Magazine—for IBM-compatible computers
PC Week—for IBM-compatible computers
Personal Computing—for all microcomputers

Many online databases such as the Computer Database, Microcomputer Index, and Microsearch index these publications.[1]

Once one decides *what* to purchase, then one must decide *where* to purchase. There are several options in addition to the local computer store. University or hospital purchasing agents may have arrangements with specified vendors for purchasing equipment at discounted prices. Computer user groups can sometimes provide special discounted prices for members. For some peripherals, such as videodisc players, audiovisual equipment suppliers may be the primary source. For other peripheral equipment, such as CD-ROM players and modems, the software producer may be a good source.

Buying all the equipment from a single source, though not always the least expensive option, can be advantageous, especially for the librarian with minimal computer expertise. Request that the supplier put all of the pieces together (circuit boards, *memory chips*, etc.) and provide simple instructions about cable connections. Dealing with a single source simplifies service arrangements. If problems arise, there is one person or organization committed to making the entire system work and responsible for all of the parts sold. Having one supplier eliminates the problem of one vendor claiming that technical problems are caused by another vendor's equipment.

Buying Tips for Specific Types of Equipment

Microcomputer technology is changing rapidly. At the time this is written, IBM's *OS/2* operating system and the NeXT computer are available, but not yet predominant. Other industry leaders have announced the Extended Industry Standard Architecture (EISA) as a competitor to IBM's *Micro Channel* Architecture (MCA). Apple continues to introduce faster Macintoshes with more features. With these changes occurring, librarians should select equipment after reading reviews, identifying equipment and operating systems supported by software of interest to library users, exploring software stores, and scanning the current microcomputer literature.

Macintosh and IBM-compatible microcomputers are the predominant equipment supported at this time. There are fewer decisions to make when purchasing Macintosh equipment since there are fewer configuration options. Therefore, most of the following comments refer to IBM-compatible equipment. Although the specific information presented will quickly become out of date, the basic points made are important to consider when purchasing equipment.

Central Processing Unit
Once the decision to purchase a microcomputer is made, one must consider equipment features such as processing speed, processing power, and internal architecture.

Processor: 8088, 286, 386, 486, 80286, 80386, 68000, 68030, XT, or AT

This refers to the *processor* chip. The 8088, XT, and the 286, or AT, are in older technology; the 386 and 486 technologies are newer and can support faster processing speeds. The Macintosh uses the 68000 processor for the Plus and SE, and a faster 68030 for the Macintosh SE/30 and II series. The processor should not be the sole selection criterion. Processor type along with other features indicates the overall computing power.

Processing speed: 10, 16, 20, 25, 35 *MHz*

The higher the number, the faster the processing operates. Faster processing means less time to wait for a system to *"boot up"* or for a spell-checking program to complete its task.

Bit: 8, 16, 32

This indicates the numbers of *bits*, the computer's basic unit of information, that can be processed at one time. The higher the number, the more and the faster information can be processed.

Especially with the *central processing unit* (CPU), one should consider future needs. More powerful, faster microcomputers will cost significantly more than slower ones, but the additional investment may mean that the equipment will be used longer. Purchase the most powerful microcomputer you can afford that supports the software you will be using. If you buy more than one microcomputer, consider purchasing a combination of more powerful and less powerful microcomputers with different capabilities. You will be able to provide more stations while still providing more powerful capabilities for the applications that need them. Purchasing a variety of microcomputers is not recommended for classroom environments where consistency is important.

Internal Memory

RAM: 640K, 1MB, 2MB, 4MB, 16MB

The earlier maximum amount of internal memory or random access memory (*RAM*) supported by DOS was 640K. Newer microcomputers and more powerful software (Microsoft Windows) and operating systems (OS/2) require several megabytes of memory. A microcomputer may be equipped with one amount of RAM, but be able to have memory added at a later date. The ability to add RAM is a desirable feature.

Disk Drives

Floppy disk drives: 5.25" drives (360K, 1.2MB or HD)
                    3.5" drives (720K, 800K, 1.4MB or HD)

The trend is toward the 3.5" *floppy disk* drive. Purchase the high density (*HD*) or 1.4MB drive, which can read and format the lower density disks. Lower density drives cannot read and format in high density mode. Similarly, if purchasing 5.25" disk drives, also purchase the high density or 1.2MB drives so that users can use both types of floppy disks. Providing both 3.5" and 5.25" drives allows the greatest flexibility and is recommended for at least one microcomputer until the 3.5" format is used exclusively. Some disks that have been formatted for 360K (lower density) using a high density drive cannot be used in all 360K disk drives. Check the compatibility of the different equipment configurations that will be available to users.

Macintosh computers usually have one 3.5" 800K or 1.4MB drive; other drives may be added. An additional 3.5" drive is important if a hard disk is unavailable. An *external* 5.25" drive may also be useful for those who want to transfer files from an *MS DOS* 5.25" environment to the Macintosh environment. The Macintosh FDHD SuperDrive 3.5" drives that can read and write MS-DOS, OS/2, and *ProDOS* disks, as well as Macintosh disks, are useful for transferring files from one environment to another. The type of drive to purchase depends upon the predominating floppy disk format.

Hard disks: size (40 MB, 130MB, 300MB, 2 *giga*bytes)
       access time (65, 38, 16 MS)

The larger the number for size, the more capacity is available to store programs and data on the *hard disk*. Hard disks are becoming a standard feature on all microcomputers. Unless the microcomputer is to be used for a local area network file server, the hard disk probably only needs to be about 40MB. Determining the necessary storage capacity of the hard disk depends on the space required by the software and files to be stored.

The *access time*, in milliseconds (MS), indicates how quickly information is retrieved from the hard disk. The smaller the number, the faster the access time. The larger hard disks have faster access times and are more expensive. Connecting a hard disk through a *SCSI port* (Small Computer System Interface, pronounced "scuzzy") on the microcomputer may also provide faster access time than using a hard disk controller *card*. SCSI ports provide greater flexibility in adding more hard disk capacity.

Internal Slots

Individual microcomputer makes and models have different numbers of internal *slots* for adding circuit boards needed for components and peripherals, including disk drives, CD-ROM drives, and many other parts. For example, a Macintosh SE has only one slot available for changing the standard configuration, while the Macintosh IIx has six slots. Decide on the desired configuration of the microcomputer (type of monitor, hard disk, number and type of disk drives) and all the peripherals (printer, CD-ROM drive, videodisc player, modem). Many of these devices are supported by a port directly connected to the *mother board* so they will not require a slot for a board. For example, the early IBM PCs required a disk drive controller card while the IBM PS/2 disk drives connect directly to the mother board. The Macintosh architecture also includes support for its standard configuration, as well as many ports for other devices and capabilities including printers, sound, and networking, so the one slot available on a Macintosh SE is usually adequate. Make certain that the microcomputer you purchase can support everything you want. Besides being confusing to the user, the "all-purpose" microcomputer may not be able to support all the peripherals wanted.

The number of slots available may be important in determining the type of peripheral equipment to purchase. For example, the microcomputer may not have enough slots for an *internal* modem, but could support an external modem connected to a *serial port.*

The type of microcomputer also determines the type of boards that can be used. For example, a board used in an early model IBM PC will not fit into the IBM PS/2 microchannel architecture, nor the Macintosh architecture. When ordering peripherals or other individual components, make sure to specify the microcomputer with which it will be used so that the proper components will be provided.

Number of Microcomputers

The number of microcomputers is usually determined by space and budget available, rather than ideal user-per-station ratios. Existing facilities in health sciences libraries have provided satisfactory service using the following ratios.

Example

A medical school library providing educational and *productivity software* has five Macintosh SEs and two interactive video stations for approximately 500 medical students and 200 house staff. Other public access microcomputer facilities are available in the medical center.

Example

A medium-sized teaching hospital library providing end-user searching and a CD-ROM MEDLINE workstation has three IBM PCs and one Macintosh for its 2,000 physicians, 2,500 nurses, and 200 medical residents.

Example

An academic health sciences library providing educational and productivity software has 13 IBM compatibles, 15 Macintoshes, and 10 Apple IIe's for its 1,800 students, 800 faculty, 800 volunteer faculty, and 5,500 staff.

Monitors

The main options in monitors for IBM-compatible microcomputers are
- monochrome
- mono graphics
- *CGA* (color graphics)
- *EGA* (enhanced color graphics)
- *VGA* (video graphics)

Resolution of the image increases from CGA to EGA to VGA. Monochrome monitors give better resolution than CGA monitors, but do not provide color or graphics capabilities. Buy monitors with color and graphics since more and more software is taking advantage of those features. Medically oriented educational software often uses graphics and color. Even some office application software, like word processing and spreadsheets, are easier to use with color monitors. CGA monitors provide color graphics display, but the text images are inferior. The IBM PS/2 models use VGA monitors, which provide high-quality text and graphics. One should consider VGA monitors as a first option. In some microcomputers, the monitor requires that a card be installed; in other microcomputers, the monitor connector is built into the mother board (is "on-board"). When purchasing monitors, determine all cables needed and where they will be connected.

The built-in Macintosh SE monitor provides very high resolution graphics, though not in color. External color and larger, high-resolution monochrome monitors and video display cards can be attached to Macintosh SEs and IIs.

Mice

IBM PS/2 and Macintosh models come equipped with a mouse. As more and more software includes a mouse-interface, it should be standard equipment with all microcomputer purchases. There are *bus* mice that attach to a board in the CPU; serial mice that attach to the serial port; and one-button, two-button, and three-button mice. Make sure the mouse selected is compatible with the software to be used.

Printers

There are two main types of printers to consider: dot matrix and laser. *Daisy wheel* printers also produce letter-quality output, but are not recommended because of their more limited capabilities for providing graphics or font changes. Printers connect to the serial or *parallel port* of the microcomputer. Macintosh printers connect through the AppleTalk port. The following summarizes the features of dot-matrix and laser printers.

Dot matrix (9-pin, 24-pin, *inkjet*)
  32–239 characters per second, text and graphics, near letter quality, $229–$1,999[2]

Laser (*PostScript* and non-PostScript)
  4.1–21.5 pages per minute, text and graphics, letter quality, $1,899–$19,500[3]

Within these two categories, there are numerous manufacturers and models and, as suggested by the price ranges, numerous features and capabilities. Word processing users, especially, will want high-quality output printers. Examine the most recently published comparative printer reviews. An inexpensive 9-pin dot matrix may be adequate, if high-quality word processing products are not a priority.

Noise may be a major deciding factor in libraries where the printer will not be placed in a separate room. Laser printers are fast and quiet. Currently they are expensive compared to other printers, but as less expensive models become available they may be a good option. Although inkjet printers might not be the first choice in other situations, they usually are a less expensive option than laser printers for quiet places. However, the cost of supplies and durability for high-use areas can be significant factors. Examples of inkjet printers include Canon BJ-130, Diconix 300 and 300W, and Hewlett-Packard ThinkJet, DeskJet Plus, and DeskWriter. Another option for reducing printer noise is to use printer hoods that buffer sound, though they are often cumbersome to use.

Don't forget to add the cost of supplies in determining the type of printer to purchase. Inkjet cartridges and laser printer toner cartridges are typically more expensive than dot-matrix ribbons.

The type of microcomputer and software to be used are also factors in choosing printers. Hewlett-Packard and Epson printers are usually used with IBM-compatible microcomputers. Apple's ImageWriter and Laser-Writer are most easily interfaced with Macintoshes. The Apple LaserWriter can be used with MS-DOS software, such as WordPerfect for word processing, that has the appropriate printer *drivers*. Make sure that the library's software is compatible with the printer being considered. Look for industry standards by identifying printers supported by software and printers emulated by other printers. The printers mentioned most frequently may be a good purchase decision since they will probably be well-supported by a wide variety of software. In 1989, the standard printer *emulations* for IBM-compatible microcomputers were Apple LaserWriter, IBM Graphics, IBM Proprinter, Epson, Diablo, or Hewlett-Packard LaserJet.[4]

The number of printers required depends upon the software applications being used. For end-user searching, one printer per station may be needed. For word processing and other productivity software, fewer printers are required since printing a document consumes a short time as compared to creating the document. Sharing printers among a cluster of workstations or dedicating certain stations for printing only is a cost-effective approach to providing printers. In a small facility or when user convenience is of primary importance, then one printer per station may be desirable. When workstations are located throughout the library, more printers are required. For many educational programs, printers are only occasionally required. Local area networks reduce the need for printers required since networked printers can be easily shared.

Example

In an academic health sciences library, 3 laser printers, 1 near-letter quality printer, and 50 dot matrix printers are available for 10 Apple IIe, 24 Macintosh, and 25 IBM stations. The facility includes a classroom and provides access to productivity software, database searching, and educational software.

Example

In an academic health sciences library, 2 laser printers are available for 12 networked IBM workstations and 3 dot-matrix printers are available for stand-alone stations. The majority of the use of this facility is for educational materials with only some users given access to productivity tools.

Example

In a teaching hospital library with an IBM AT and a Macintosh SE, a dot-matrix printer was provided for each station. The microcomputers are used for both educational software and word processing.

Example

In an academic health sciences library, three dot-matrix printers are available, one each for IBM, Macintosh, and Apple IIe users. The facility includes 29 IBM, 21 Macintosh, and 8 Apple IIe stations. The facility provides productivity and educational software.

Printer *switch boxes* and debit or credit card readers are printer-related devices that may be useful in libraries. There are a variety of printer switch box devices, the simplest of which consists of an A/B switch to direct printing from either of two microcomputers (A or B) to one printer. Some printers, such as laser printers, may not function properly with manual switch boxes. Check with manufacturers on use of the switch with a specific printer to avoid possible equipment damage. More sophisticated switch boxes include *buffers* that can store print jobs and direct printing from five or more stations to one printer by queueing print jobs without requiring users to flip switches.

Although most libraries provide free dot-matrix printing, many libraries charge for laser printing. One way to collect fees is through debit or credit card devices similar to those attached to photocopy machines. If the library uses photocopy cards, then contact the company that supplies them to see if these devices are available for laser or other printers. A separate system may be advisable if the accounting and charging schemes are different from the photocopy system. Products from XCP, Inc., are used by some health sciences libraries for debit-card control of laser printer output.

Modems

Most medical librarians are well-versed on the options for modems or can easily get advice. As a very brief review, the main options are: (1) internal or external and (2) baud rate, currently 1200 to 2400. Internal modems have the advantage of being installed inside the microcomputer, secured and out of the way. External modems, which are attached to the microcomputer's serial port, have the advantage of being easily moved from one microcomputer to another, including from an IBM-compatible to a Macintosh, though a different cable is required. Transmission speed for modems and telephone lines is increasing. Purchase the modem with the fastest baud rate widely used, 2400 baud at the time this was written. Some very high speed modems are available but are primarily used for internal networks and are not supported by commercial database vendors. Software is also a consideration when buying modems. For example, some Hayes-compatible modems did not work with early versions of Grateful Med.

CD-ROM Drives

There are many options for CD-ROM drives in this burgeoning field: individual external and internal drives, stacked multiple drives for use on a single workstation or shared through a local area network. CD-ROM drives require either a circuit board in the microcomputer or connection to the microcomputer's SCSI port.

The software used should determine the type of equipment to be purchased. The software distributor may also be a good source for equipment. Some distributors offer leasing plans, which may be advantageous with this changing technology. Cost/space, security, and user access to the CD-ROM disks are also issues in determining the appropriate CD-ROM drive to buy. Stacked multiple drives can provide easy access to multiple CD-ROM disks with little or no staff involvement. However, they are more expensive than a single drive. Internal CD-ROM drives don't take up user work space, but may cause people to be confused about which drive (floppy disk or CD-ROM) to use.

Interactive Videodisc Equipment

Interactive videodisc, which combines computer interaction with videodisc images, is an area of increasing importance in health sciences education, but is not widely written about in the popular microcomputer literature. Interactive videodisc requires a videodisc player and a monitor. The monitor must be either one that can overlay computer output onto videodisc images or a separate one for videodisc images used in addition to the microcomputer monitor.

Although interactive videodisc technology has existed for many years, it is still relatively undeveloped because applications have been limited. Even de facto standards have not been established, though the Pioneer LDV 6000 series videodisc player is well-supported, and the IBM InfoWindow display has growing support. Macintosh interactive video is also developing. However, specific software applications must be the primary factor in determining interactive videodisc equipment requirements. Libraries committed to providing interactive videodisc programs may have to establish several stations, each with different equipment. For example, one medium-sized academic medical library has three interactive video stations, each with different equipment configurations to support interactive video programs with different equipment requirements.

Projection Systems

Video projectors, color LCD video projectors, and overhead projector data displays are important pieces of equipment for group instruction and are also discussed in Chapter Three (Planning Facilities). Video projectors usually provide large displays in color with clearer images. Data displays are placed on an overhead projector to project primarily monochrome images, though color displays such as those by nView Corporation have been announced. The image size depends on the distance the overhead projector is from the screen, although the size is usually smaller than from a video projector. A good quality overhead projector that stays cool is required for the data displays to operate most effectively. LCD video projectors use similar technology for the data display, but include a projection system eliminating the need for the overhead projector. The Kodak LC500 is the first example of this type of projector. Video projectors typically cost from $8,000 to more than $16,000; LCD video projectors are approximately $3,500; and data displays are approximately $1,600. Most video projectors can also be used for big-screen videocassette projection and can be mounted out of the way on the ceiling. LCD video projectors and data displays are much more portable.

All of these displays are connected to the microcomputer through the monitor port, that is, the connector to which the monitor usually attaches to the microcomputer. These devices require graphics output, for example, CGA, EGA, VGA, or Macintosh output, in either monochrome or high resolution color.

The type of monitor output from the microcomputer that is attached to the projector is the major factor in determining which video projector or data display to purchase. For example, the Sony 1031Q supports EGA graphics, while its earlier 1020Q supports only CGA graphics. Projectors that can support higher resolution outputs usually can support lower resolution outputs as well, but the reverse may not be true. For example, a Kodak DataShow supports CGA graphics, but a Kodak DataShow HR is required for EGA graphics. Some data display devices, like the nView 2 + II, can support a variety of outputs from CGA to VGA to Macintosh II color resolution.

The data displays and LCD video projectors are specifically designed to attach directly to microcomputers. Different cables and connectors may be required to support different types of microcomputers. Most video projectors are multipurpose and require a computer interface device, for example, an Extron *RGB* 102E Computer Display Interface device to convert the computer image to input for the video projector. Different interface device models are needed for different types of microcomputers, such as IBM compatibles, Macintosh SE, and the Macintosh Plus.

Before purchase, test the projection devices with the microcomputer to be used and the software to be projected. Make sure the device provides a clear image, large enough for the intended group size. Some problems with early models of the data displays were

- overheating after being on for a long time causing the image to disappear
- distorted images because the device screen dimensions were in a different proportion from the microcomputer monitor's screen

- inability to show shades of gray, so that some color combinations would appear all black or all white

Large screen television-type monitors are an alternative to projection systems though they usually provide a smaller image. Thus, they are only adequate for groups of five to seven students. Only those monitors that have computer input connectors can be used.

Supplies and Miscellaneous Equipment

Printer ribbons or cartridges and printer paper need to be kept on hand. Check the printer specifications to determine the type of supplies required. In addition to local computer stores and office and library supplies stores and catalogs, there are many computer supplies catalogs, such as those from Misco, Global Computer Supplies, and Thomas Computer Corporation. In the examples below, indicating levels of supplies used, one box of paper includes 2,500 sheets.

Example

One academic medical library with three dot-matrix printers for 31 microcomputers uses one box of paper and two ribbons per printer per month. Two laser printers also are available that use two reams of paper and two cartridges per printer per month. Dot-matrix printing is free. Laser printouts are charged at 10 cents per page. The facility provides productivity and educational software.

Example

A hospital library has one dot-matrix printer for its one workstation that supports both CD-ROM databases and productivity software and uses one-half box of paper and two ribbons per month.

Example

A teaching hospital library with four workstations for productivity software and CD-ROM and database searching uses one-half box of paper and one ribbon per month per printer for its three printers.

Example

An academic health sciences library with three dot-matrix printers for 58 workstations for productivity and educational software uses one box of paper and three ribbons per printer per month.

Example

An academic medical library with three printers for three workstations for CD-ROM and online database searching uses one-half box of paper and two inkjet cartridges per printer per month.

Surge protector power outlet strips or other power conditioning equipment is important because microcomputer equipment is very susceptible to power surges and brownouts. Lack of power conditioning can lead to equipment damage and data loss. The surge protectors should be adequate for the wattage of the equipment plugged into them.

If mouse devices are provided, their action is improved by *mouse pads,* which are a better surface for rolling than a slick table top.

Antiglare screen guards can make the use of microcomputers more comfortable.

Security devices also should be considered. Typically, libraries address security issues by securing the computer equipment to the workstation. There are numerous locking devices and ways of attaching computer equipment to the furniture. Some computer furniture is designed to house equipment securely, as described in Chapter Three (Planning Facilities). Some security cables are wrapped around a carrel or table leg. Other devices need to be adhered or bolted to the work surface. A few sample security device manufacturers include Compu-Gard, Doss Industries, and FMJ.

Security devices with keys for locking down the device, turning on the power, or unlocking the keyboard must be attached so that the locks are easily reached. Quick access to the equipment for repair and maintenance is important, especially if the library is charged for the time a repair person spends releasing the equipment in order to work on it. The security device should also be easily accessed so that the equipment can be removed or relocated if necessary. Security measures should also protect against theft of internal parts such as modems, memory chips, and circuit boards.

Upgrading and Replacing Equipment

Microcomputers are not one-time-only investments, nor do they have the longevity of use of typewriters or media equipment. Although the equipment may still be in good condition after five years, it may need to be replaced because of advances in technology. The microcomputer industry has seen major innovative developments approximately every five years. Keeping up with the technology is a major issue for libraries. Libraries do not need to—and probably cannot afford to—replace equipment with every advance. Addition or replacement of equipment such as circuit boards, monitors, RAM chips, *coprocessors,* hard disks, and even mother boards (the main circuit board) can upgrade the equipment between major purchases. Some upgrades may require other changes, different memory chips or increased power supplies, for example. Other upgrades may be able to utilize some of the old components, such as *network boards* and modems.

Eventually new and more technologically advanced equipment will be needed, but older equipment may still be useful for some applications. If there is room, add to rather than replace old equipment. Some vendors may offer trade-in programs to offset some of the cost of new equipment. For libraries with large microcomputer facilities, equipment replacement can be on a continuous cycle with some of the equipment replaced every year. As a result, public access facilities would always have a mix of old and new equipment, but over time older equipment would be replaced. Such a facility is more difficult to manage since many different types of equipment are available for public use. However, a piecemeal process may be necessary since funds for replacement equipment may be even more difficult to get than funds to develop new facilities.

Classroom equipment should not be replaced in stages. To facilitate training, identical equipment is required in a classroom; all the equipment needs to be replaced at one time.

SETTING UP EQUIPMENT FOR USERS

Once the microcomputer equipment is delivered, it must be set up for use. The following guidelines may be useful.

Store Equipment in a Secure, Dry Place

If the equipment cannot be put into the public area immediately, make certain that it will not be damaged or stolen in the interim. Stored equipment may be more easily stolen because it is usually not in a visible or monitored area.

Keep Packing Materials

Keep at least one box and its packing materials for each kind of item until the equipment has been fully tested. If there is a defect in the equipment, the original box and packing material will be needed to return the item for repair or replacement.

Keep Warranty Information

As with any type of equipment, warranty cards included in the box should be completed and returned to the manufacturer and a copy retained. Packing lists provided by the manufacturer may include serial numbers or other warranty information.

Equipment Installation

To set up the equipment, complete these tasks:
- install boards such as internal modems and CD-ROM driver boards
- install system enhancements such as additional RAM chips and coprocessor chips
- connect peripherals
- plug in power cords
- run equipment diagnostics or tests to make certain the equipment is working properly
- install the operating system
- format hard disks
- secure the equipment
- prepare it for public use

These tasks can be performed in-house or by vendors, depending on the staff's availability and technical expertise.

Preparing the equipment for use requires library staff to learn about the equipment, its components, and how it operates. With this knowledge, the staff will be more able to handle subsequent problems or modifications. Also, the do-it-yourself approach assures that the tasks are completed. These tasks require information gleaned from manuals, manufacturer technical support hot-lines, the institution's computer support technicians, or the technically expert, helpful user.

Equipment installation is not simple or obvious. A part might fit the slot or connector, but may not operate. Putting RAM chips in the wrong direction just means the board will not work (though it may cause much frustration trying to determine *why* it does not work). Attaching a CD-ROM cable to the wrong port on the computer could cause equipment damage.

The other approach is to have the vendor prepare the equipment for use, except for attaching the monitor, keyboard, and mouse to the CPU; securing the equipment; and plugging in the electrical power cords. Request specific instructions about which cable goes where if necessary.

PREPARING EQUIPMENT FOR PUBLIC USE

Several steps are needed to make microcomputers more "user friendly," less prone to destruction by users, and easier for staff to maintain.

Describe the Workstation

Inform users of the configuration of the workstation, peripherals attached, and any other features. This is helpful information since different software has different equipment requirements. For example, a small label attached either to the microcomputer or the workstation might read

IBM PS/2 Model 50
1MB RAM
3.5" high density drive
5.25" high density drive
40MB hard disk
dot-matrix printer

Name the Workstation

If there are several microcomputer workstations available, give each one a name or number to identify it. There is less confusion if one says "I have a problem at PC1," or reports that "the monitor does not work on PC5," than if one says "the PC over in the corner by the drinking fountain doesn't work." Names can be 1, 2, 3, A, B, C, or Alice, Joe, and Mary—anything as long as each is unique.

Provide User Instructions

The novice user needs some basic information to get started including
- where to find the on/off switch
- which drive is Drive A, which is B, which is C
- how to insert a floppy disk
- the sequence of steps to get a program started

Similar instructions are needed for other equipment such as printers and CD-ROM players.

Prepare the Hard Disk

More and more microcomputers are purchased with hard disks. They make it easier to provide software to users and are necessary for the operation of some very large software programs. But, hard disks do require special attention since it is easy for users to wreak havoc with them. Suggestions for avoiding problems for DOS and Macintosh microcomputers are included in the following sections. However, operating system versions change and new software replaces old, so consider these suggestions as general approaches and look for similar solutions using current operating systems and utility software. To safeguard against damage, always have *backup copies* of software or backup copies of the entire hard disk with software fully installed.

Hard Disk Management for MS-DOS Microcomputers

An understanding of the operating system is very useful, so read articles, books, and especially the DOS manual. In general, (1) create *subdirectories* for different software programs, including DOS; (2) keep only the files necessary for start-up in the *root directory* (for example, the *AUTOEXEC.BAT* and *CONFIG.SYS* files); and (3) include a path in the AUTOEXEC.BAT file to make DOS and any other universally important files available from any subdirectory.

There are different approaches to maintaining software on hard disks. If not prevented, users will make changes to software on hard disks, either deliberately or inadvertently. An open approach to maintaining software provides more flexibility to users, but requires continual monitoring by library staff to keep software in good working condition. In some situations, once the hard disk has been configured and the software installed, librarians will be loath to repeat the process. One way to protect against unwanted modifications is to use security software that controls access to the software on the disk. This software allows only an authorized user, for example, the librarian, to add and delete software. Others can use the software but cannot copy, delete, or modify it. Some examples of this type of software are Secret Disk II, Hands-off-the-Program, and HDCopy.

Another, less expensive approach to security is to use DOS commands. DOS does not provide all the sophisticated features of security software, but it may prevent many common problems. For example, a common mistake for the novice user is to issue a format command without specifying which drive contains the disk to be formatted. This causes the hard disk to be reformatted and erases all the existing programs and files. Inadvertent reformatting of the hard disk is easily avoided by using the *RENAME command* to change the name of the DOS format command. A batch file called FORMAT.BAT that includes a floppy drive specification can then provide users the format function by its familiar name, as illustrated below.

Procedure for avoiding hard disk reformatting using DOS ver. 3.3:

1. Rename FORMAT command to NEW

   C>RENAME FORMAT.COM NEW.COM

2. Create a batch file called "Format" using the renamed FORMAT command

   C>COPY CON FORMAT.BAT   (copying input from the "console" or keyboard into a batch file called FORMAT.BAT)

   C>NEW A: (where NEW is the new name of FORMAT.COM)

   (Ctrl) Z   (ending the batch file)

With these modifications, when the FORMAT command is specified, the batch file will instruct the computer to format a disk in drive A:.

DOS provides solutions to other problems such as: (1) users erasing or modifying program files, making the software unusable; (2) users copying into the root directory of the hard disk their own software including an AUTOEXEC.BAT file that automatically starts up their software and replaces the AUTOEXEC.BAT file created by the library; and, (3) users storing their own files on the hard disk, taking up hard disk space. Using the DOS utility *ATTRIB* (Attribute) to make the attributes of files "read only" means they cannot be modified, erased, or replaced. Files can also be hidden, making them available for use but not visible to someone issuing the DIRECTORY command.

If the original AUTOEXEC.BAT file on the root directory is readable only, it cannot be replaced; this prevents a user from copying a new AUTOEXEC.BAT file into the root directory. If all library and system files are "read only," then deleting unwanted user files is accomplished easily by using a DELETE *.* command within each subdirectory. Only users' files will be erased, since they have not been changed to "read only." A few software programs require users to write to the program files, so software should be carefully tested to make sure this procedure of creating "read only" files does not inhibit use of the software. Using these ordinary DOS commands will not prevent the knowledgeable user from maliciously causing problems, but it should prevent most of the problems inadvertently caused by novice users.

DOS versions change, and different operating systems like OS/2 and user interfaces like Microsoft's Windows provide different approaches to maintaining the hard disk in the manner desired by the library. The same type of problems may prevail, though the actual procedures and commands may change.

Once software is installed on hard disks, users need easy access to it. There are many *menu* programs that help users identify what is on the hard disk and start up the selected program with ease. Menu systems also can incorporate simple DOS commands like FORMAT and DIRECTORY. Some menu systems are *RAM-resident* and can take control as soon as the user exits a program, returning the user to the menu. Two examples of such programs are Power Menus and LANShell.

When computer literacy is an objective, librarians may choose to require users to use DOS commands to access software and start it up. This should be a conscious decision rather than one enforced by default.

Macintosh Hard Disk Management

As with MS-DOS environments, librarians can approach Macintosh hard disk management either as a nonrestrictive, open environment or one that limits the user's ability to make modifications to suit individual preferences. The first approach gives more power to the user, but requires frequent monitoring by library staff to maintain the integrity of the software. The second approach requires more initial set-up time and restricts some user options, but it results in an environment that is easier to maintain. The following procedures may be useful for those interested in a more restrictive approach to hard disk management on the Macintosh.

Macintosh hard disk management employs the same principles as the MS-DOS environment. The *system tools* can create separate *system folders* and folders for each different program or application to avoid cluttering up the first level of the desktop space. Folders within folders can organize the hard disk and help lead users quickly to the software needed (similar to subdirectories and menus in MS-DOS environments).

CHOOSER is a *desk accessory* used to set configurations, such as sound level and mouse tracking speed, to individual specifications. Most of the CHOOSER elements, including General, Keyboard, and Mouse, can be thrown into the Macintosh *trash* once they have been set to prevent users from changing the configurations. Some CHOOSER elements, such as Monitor and Sound, must be retained so that changes can be made for different software specifications. For example, when a color monitor is available, users must switch the monitor configuration to color from black/white for certain software and back to black/white for others.

The Macintosh System Tools through version 6.0.2 do not include a way to protect files. However, other utility programs, like MacTools included in Copy II Mac and ResEdit, not only protect programs from user modification and erasure but also from copying. As with the DOS ATTRIB utility, these utilities make it possible to protect and hide program files. Files that are hidden are available for use but cannot be seen by the user. The main *icon* file for the program should be protected, but not hidden. If it is not protected, the entire folder within which the program resides can be thrown in the trash and erased. If it is hidden, users cannot see it to start the application. The entire system folder can be hidden. These techniques allow you to set up the hard disk once and not have to worry about users destroying your efforts. With protected library and system files, user files can easily be purged from the hard disk by selecting ALL from the Apple Edit menu and trashing the entire system folder. Protected files cannot be removed; only the users' unprotected files will be erased.

PREVENTIVE MAINTENANCE AND REPAIR

There are many books about maintenance, common equipment problems, and repair for those who have the staff and time to become involved in these activities.

Basic preventive maintenance of microcomputers is quick and easy and can prevent problems from occurring. This includes
- keeping the workstations in a clean environment, away from food, beverages, smoke, and dust
- cleaning the workstations as needed by wiping monitors, dusting keyboards and other surfaces, and using a disk drive head cleaner

Repairs should be infrequent since electronic equipment has few mechanical parts. However, common problems are with (1) disk drives that get out of alignment, (2) monitors that flicker, waver, or go completely blank, and (3) processor chips that are defective.

Maintenance contracts are an option. Cost is a key consideration. Maintenance contracts in a major metropolitan area are typically 10 percent of the original equipment price on an annual basis for carry-in service. The experience of several academic medical libraries with large public access facilities indicates that maintenance contracts often cost more than the individual repairs would have cost. For libraries with few microcomputers, other factors may make maintenance contracts desirable. For those with minimal computer expertise on staff, having on-site trouble-shooting and repair assistance is invaluable. A contract can guarantee a maximum response time, for example, "repair or replace within 24 hours" or provide loaner equipment so that downtime is minimal. There is always the risk that the repair will involve a major expenditure. For example, replacing an IBM PS/2 Model 50 mother board costs $800, and replacing a Macintosh disk drive costs $300. Some equipment, such as the Macintosh, requires authorized repair services, so do-it-yourself repairs are very risky. Some equipment like laser printers, whose most typical repairs are expensive, may warrant maintenance contracts, especially if the equipment is used heavily.

The parent institution may have in-house repair services that are free or relatively inexpensive. Or it may have an institution-wide contract for computer repair. Libraries with large microcomputer facilities may need additional staff to identify problems and make simple repairs, such as replacing a defective disk drive or modem board.

Virus Protection

Computer *viruses* are programs that are designed to replicate themselves onto disks, thereby spreading the infection. In their most malignant forms, they can destroy or alter data or program files. In their most benign forms, they can cause happy faces to appear or say "Gotcha!" Hard disks provide the main mechanisms for infecting new disks, since once a hard disk is infected it can spread the virus to any floppy disk used with it. However, viruses can also spread when files are copied from one floppy disk to another. Macintosh environments seem to be more susceptible to viruses than the MS-DOS environments, though health sciences libraries have had both types of environments infected.

Using illegally copied software is the most common means of becoming infected with a virus. If you acquire software from *bulletin boards* and other suppliers of *public domain software*, make sure the software is screened for viruses. Using commercial software greatly reduces the possibility of virus infection. However, public access facilities are especially vulnerable to viruses since they have many different users operating in a fairly unrestricted manner.

Computer *vaccine* programs can be installed on hard disks. Some vaccines are *memory resident* and can check for viruses when an application program is used. With other vaccines or virus detectors, users can run the program to check for viruses on a specific disk. Several vaccine programs are necessary since different programs usually check for different viruses. You should continually check hard disks for virus infection and delete all infected files. In extreme cases, the entire hard disk may need to be reformatted and uninfected software reinstalled. This is why backup procedures are essential. Weekly checks may be sufficient; more frequent checks are necessary when there is evidence of virus infection. Constant vigilance will confine the spread of infection. There are no foolproof measures for protecting against viruses. Clever programmers can always create new viruses that escape detection, at least until another programmer creates a program to detect it. New vaccines or new versions of vaccines will continually need to be installed to protect against new viruses.[5,6]

SUMMARY

In selecting microcomputer equipment, librarians must consider many factors in order to obtain equipment that is appropriate for the user and the library within the institutional environment. After purchase, equipment must be prepared for the user so that it is easy to use and easy to support. Managing equipment is an ongoing process including maintenance, repair, upgrade, and replacement.

Use figure 4.1, equipment purchase worksheet, as you decide on each equipment component and how many to purchase. Multiply by unit cost to determine the total cost. Don't forget to include tax and shipping. For examples of some equipment costs, see Chapter Three (Planning Facilities).

Figure 4.1 Equipment Purchase Worksheet

Description	Cost per unit	Units	Total
Microcomputer Model	_____	___	___
RAM	_____	___	___
Floppy Drive	_____	___	___
Hard Disk (Size)	_____	___	___
Monitor	_____	___	___
Printer	_____	___	___
Modem	_____	___	___
CD-ROM Drive	_____	___	___
Videodisc Player	_____	___	___
Videodisc Monitor	_____	___	___
Security Device	_____	___	___
Surge Protector	_____	___	___

References
1. O'Leary M. Computer databases: a survey. Part 3: product databases. Database 1987 Apr; 10(2):56–64.
2. PC Magazine printer guide: monochrome dot matrix printers. PC Magazine 1989 Nov 14;8(19):230–43.
3. PC Magazine printer guide: laser printers. PC Magazine 1989 Nov 14;8(19):105–10.
4. The 1989 printer roundup. PC Magazine 1989 Nov 14;8(19):101.
5. Clancy S. Viruses, Trojan horses, and other badware: information and implications for online searchers. Database 1988 Aug;11(4):37–44.
6. Turitz M. Macintosh computer viruses: a guide for the complete novice. Apple Library Users Group Newsletter 1989 Jul;7(3):63–70.

Additional Resources

Datapro Reports on Microcomputers. Delran, NJ: DataPro Research, 1981–. Contains equipment and software descriptions, vendor and manufacturer addresses.

Equipment Directory of Audio-Visual, Computer, and Video Products. 35th ed. Fairfax, VA: International Communications Industries Association, 1989. Contains equipment descriptions, manufacturer addresses, and retail dealers and distributors.

T.H.E. Journal (Technological Horizons in Education). Articles and advertisements provide information about equipment, software, security devices, educational computing. (Free to qualified individuals in educational institutions and training departments in the United States and Canada)

Demarais N. The librarian's CD-ROM handbook. Westport, CT: Meckler, 1989.

Further Reading

Gookin D. How to understand and buy computers. 2d ed. San Diego, CA:Computer Publishing Enterprises, 1988.

Aspinwall J, Burke R, Todd M. The PC user's survival guide. Redwood City, CA:M & T Books, 1989.

Mueller S. Upgrading and repairing PCs. Carmel, IN:Que, 1988.

Simpson A. The best book of DOS. Indianapolis, IN:HW Sams, 1989.

Naiman A, ed. The Macintosh bible: thousands of basic and advanced tips, tricks, and shortcuts. 2d ed. Berkeley, CA:Goldstein & Blair, 1988.

Lu C. The Apple Macintosh book. 3d ed. Redmond, WA:Microsoft Press, 1988.

Williams GB. Chilton's guide to Macintosh repair and maintenance. Radnor, PA: Chilton, 1986.

Chapter Five
Local Area Networks

Local area networks (LANs) are of increasing interest to libraries with public access microcomputers, especially to those with five or more workstations. There are many books describing LANs, their selection, and operation. Rather than summarize technical details described so well in other sources, this chapter focuses on practical considerations and raises issues that will require further investigation. The chapter follows the sequence of establishing a LAN including
- definition of a LAN
- advantages and disadvantages of LANs
- defining library needs and selecting a LAN
- hardware issues
- software issues
- maintaining a LAN
- costs involved

DEFINITION OF A LAN

Local area networks (LANs) provide the means to connect individual microcomputer workstations together to share software and hardware and to communicate between computers. LANs may provide network functions either through (1) a dedicated, central file server or (2) shared servers acting on a *peer-to-peer* basis, which may also be workstations on the LAN.

This chapter focuses on LANs with dedicated, central file servers since that configuration seems to be most practical for and prevalent in libraries. Dedicated file servers provide more control and easier network management, since the network functions are centralized on one server. Typically, a file server is a sophisticated microcomputer, such as a Macintosh SE/30 or an IBM-compatible microcomputer with 386 MHz processing power or whatever is the most powerful microcomputer at the time. Each microcomputer on the LAN, including the file server, contains a network interface board or has built-in network capability (as do the Macintoshes) and is connected to other microcomputers through one of a variety of wiring types—thin *Ethernet* or *twisted pair*—and one of a variety of wiring *topologies*—*token ring*, bus, or *star*. LANs generally are confined to a room, building, or department, though they may be connected to larger networks or accessible from remote locations.

ADVANTAGES OF LANS

LANs have many features that make them very desirable for public access microcomputer environments in libraries. Some features, such as sharing peripherals and conducting electronic messaging, can be provided through other means, though often with more difficulty. Because many features are unique to specific LANs, the features described here may not be available with all LANs. LANs used for staff areas and for library functions, such as online catalogs or an integrated library system, provide many other advantages that are beyond the scope of this book. As with all microcomputer technology, LAN technology is evolving rapidly; many new features will have appeared since this book went to press.

Software Control and Distribution

Many application programs, such as computer-based instruction and word processing, can be stored on the file server and distributed to workstations as files instead of circulated on disks. This method of distribution can reduce circulation workload as well as protect the library's software from loss, damage, and theft. Software that is frequently updated and has been purchased for multiple workstations is easier to maintain on a LAN, since each update can be made once on the LAN rather than many times on many different floppy disks or hard disks. As with stand-alone workstations with hard disks, LANs can provide easy access to software through menus that start up the selected software. See "Software Issues" in this chapter and Chapter Six (Software Collections) for more information about software.

Shared Peripherals

Users prefer printers, modems, and other peripherals at every workstation, but that is not feasible in most libraries. A peripheral that is a part of the LAN can be used by any workstation on the network, rather than by just the computer to which it is attached. This is especially useful when many different users need a peripheral only occasionally. The LAN can control access so that all users have equal access or some users receive priority access.

LANs provide the flexibility of maintaining some printers for use by a specific workstation only (such as a workstation dedicated to MEDLINE searching), while making other printers available on a shared basis. Printer jobs are *spooled* to the networked printer and queued for printing. The ability to share printers should not be the main reason for considering a LAN, however, since there are other, less expensive devices specifically designed for this purpose.

Modems also can be shared through a LAN. But because a modem can handle only one user at a time, there needs to be a modem on the network for each anticipated, or supported, simultaneous user. For example, MEDLINE training for five users requires five modems. However, when the training session is over, any network station can use a modem. Shared modems require communications software that can be configured to access a modem located away from the user station.

Some CD-ROM products, such as the OPTI-NET software by ONLINE Products Corporation, have been designed to operate on a network. Different CD-ROM disks can be placed in each drive, giving network users easy access to different databases such as Psyclit, PDQ, or Science Citation Index, or to different years of a single database such as MEDLINE. Reference tools, like *Books in Print*, the *PDR*, and *Ulrich's International Periodical Directory*, also are available on CD-ROM. They can be valuable resources to both users and staff, especially if they are easily accessible throughout the library via a network. Multiple users can access a single CD-ROM disk in these systems simultaneously, although there are practical limits to the number in order to maintain satisfactory response time.

Connection to Wide Area Networks

For libraries in larger institutions that have *wide area networks* connecting computers (mainframes, minis, and LANs) throughout the institution, a LAN can provide shared access to the wide area network. Linking to the institution's wide area network may, in turn, provide access to other central services, such as modem pools and communications links to other institutions. Some of these connections, such as Ethernet, provide for many simultaneous users. The system works both ways. Library LAN users can go to outside systems; users connected to the wide area network throughout the institution have access to the library LAN. The result is a potential increase in the number of both users and hours the library network can be accessed, since use would not be restricted to the hours the library is open. It is essential that the library retain control of access to its own network in such situations.

Institution-wide connections facilitate communication throughout the organization, an important factor in IAIMS-type projects. For example, in one medical school, the library LAN is connected to the institution's wide area network and provides access from within the library to the clinical information system, the locally mounted MEDLINE system, and to other services.

Shared Databases

Library databases, such as the online catalog, the serials check-in system, the books-on-order files, may be made available to all LAN users. Some database management software, like dBASE IV, and microcomputer-based integrated library systems, like those by Sydney, have network features that maintain database integrity while allowing users to search the files. A LAN can provide different levels of access to different users, so that designated library staff can update and modify the records, whereas library users can view, but not modify, the records.

Copy Protection

Although not fail-safe, especially against sophisticated computer users, LANs offer some protection against illegal copying of software. For the less sophisticated user, finding the software files to copy within the network system can be difficult, especially when a menu is the user interface. For some software, the start-up file can be made executable only through the LAN, making it impossible to copy and use outside the network.

Dial-In Access

Users may find it inconvenient to come to the library, or they may want access to the LAN after hours. Dial-in access through modems can be provided. Even at 2400 baud, telephone transmission speed is very slow, so a user cannot simply dial a LAN using typical communications software, like Smartcom or ProComm, to access and run applications software as if from a workstation on the LAN. However, using remote control software, like Carbon Copy or PC Anywhere, processing can occur on a microcomputer that is physically connected to the LAN with just the monitor's images transmitted across telephone lines to the remote microcomputer. This function requires a microcomputer on the LAN that is dedicated to processing for remote use. By limiting remote use to the hours the library is closed, the same stations could be used during the day by users in the library and after hours by users outside the library. As an alternative to providing single stations for each remote access use, multitasking software, like Novell's NetWare Access Server on a 386-style microcomputer, can provide processing power for multiple, simultaneous remote users. Remote control software also is commonly used to connect to stand-alone workstations.

File Transfer

LANs that can accommodate both Macintosh and MS DOS operating systems allow easy transfer of files from one computer environment to the other. The MS-DOS and Macintosh microcomputers will still not be able to run each other's software, but they can at least use files created in other environments. If software, such as Microsoft Word and WordPerfect, are available for both MS-DOS and Macintosh operating systems, then the software easily converts the files. Since file transfers can be achieved by other methods, this feature should not be a primary consideration for establishing a LAN, but a useful bonus.

Electronic Mail

The ability to store, send, and receive messages among users is particularly important for office LANs, but perhaps only of minor significance for a library's public access LAN. Electronic mail (E-mail) can be used for an electronic suggestion box; if individual user identification codes are established, library users can send messages to each other. E-mail can also be used to send documents to others on the LAN, for example, student reports to faculty.

DISADVANTAGES OF LANS

Establishing a local area network may be a natural next step after establishing a public access microcomputer environment, or a LAN may be an integral part of the facility from its inception. However, the decision to establish a LAN should not be made casually; LANs are not problem free, and they do have drawbacks.

Additional Cost

Depending on the type of LAN (for example, Novell, AppleShare, 3COM+, TOPS) and the type of workstation (IBM-compatible or Macintosh), the cost of a local area network can be significant. Typically, there is the cost of the microcomputer to serve as a file server, the LAN software, the LAN boards for each station including the file server, the wiring, and the wiring installation. Other costs might include a consultant for setting up the LAN and additional copies of application software or network licenses. Establishing a Macintosh LAN is usually less expensive because the Macintosh has built-in network capability eliminating the need to purchase LAN boards.

Additional Staff and Expertise

LANs generally require more sophisticated computer expertise to set up and maintain, including detailed knowledge of the microcomputer's operating system, DOS or *Finder*, and the LAN's own proprietary operating system. A consultant can help with the initial development of the LAN, but the library needs a LAN administrator for ongoing operation and maintenance. LAN administrators have a wide range of responsibilities, from checking wiring connections to designing the structure of the LAN. Just as problems occur with equipment and software on stand-alone workstations, problems arise with the addition of a LAN. Since users quickly come to rely on the LAN, network problems and enhancements must be handled immediately by a staff member who is available and capable. Chapter Eight (Personnel) outlines some of the tasks associated with network management.

Summary of Advantages and Disadvantages

It is important first to decide what is to be accomplished with a LAN and to determine whether advantages will outweigh the disadvantages. Libraries with just a few microcomputers may determine that the cost and extra staff effort are not worth the benefits.

For hospital libraries using microcomputer-based integrated library systems, the LAN is an essential component of the system, and the decision may not be whether to have a LAN, but how else to use it. One small academic medical center library has found its seven-station Novell LAN extremely valuable for providing access to the microcomputer-based catalog and serials holdings records, as well as to application software. The library has three public access stations and four library staff stations.

Several academic medical libraries with large facilities have found LANs to be invaluable, especially for software distribution; however, other similar facilities have decided LANs are too costly and require more technical expertise than is available.

SELECTING A LAN

Once you decide to establish a LAN, you then must establish specifications for the LAN including
- the number and type of stations (MS-DOS, Macintosh, or multiple types)
- the type of activity anticipated (software sharing, database development and access)
- the amount of hard disk storage space needed (based on the software to be stored on the file server)
- the number and size of the files to be stored
- other features desired (remote dial-in access, wide area network connection)

This list can be used to compare different LANs and to make certain that any LAN selected matches the specifications required.

In selecting a LAN, consider one factor above all others: its *connectivity* to other computer resources in the institution. LAN selection should not be made independently if the library is part of a larger institution. If the institution already has established one type of LAN elsewhere, then that is the LAN to establish within the library. If one type of LAN is more compatible with the institution's wide area network, then it should be the network of choice. It is essential, of course, to be certain that library-specific needs can be met by the LAN, compromised, or handled in some other way.

If selection is left to the library, then the usual selection criteria prevail: features, costs, and support. LANs are a complex subject, and it is easy for sales representatives to overwhelm buyers with detailed technical descriptions. Some basic understanding of LANs is very valuable; the list of recommended readings at the end of the chapter is a resource for more information. The LAN market leader, as identified in journal articles or other industry reports, may be a good option since, in addition to being preferred by a large mass of buyers, it may also have more third-party software and hardware options for enhancing the LAN. In 1989, Novell NetWare had the major share of the LAN market for IBM-compatibles.

After a LAN is selected, librarians must keep informed about their constant revisions and the new software programs and equipment options being developed to enhance performance and add features. For example, early in Novell LAN development, network printers had to be directly connected to the file server in order to be shared. However, in later developments of third-party software, such as LANSpool, printers connected to individual workstations could be shared, thereby increasing the number of printers available for use in perhaps more convenient locations.

EQUIPMENT ISSUES

The equipment required depends upon the network selected. For example, the network boards (such as Ethernet, *ARCNET*, token ring) and cabling (*coaxial*, twisted pair) are often specified by the LAN. When a choice exists, connectivity and compatibility with institution-wide standards again should be the overriding consideration.

File Server

The type of equipment required for a LAN file server is defined by the type of LAN. AppleShare requires a Macintosh (such as a Macintosh SE/30 or II series); Novell NetWare can run on most IBM-compatible microcomputers (such as a 386- or 486-style microcomputer). Some LANs have proprietary file servers that are either optional or mandatory.

When purchasing a microcomputer for a file server, look for one that provides the most processing power, as described in Chapter Four (Equipment and Peripherals). Additional RAM, 4MB, for example, can speed up network service by allowing disk *caching*. The file server can then store frequently used files in RAM, where they are more quickly accessed than files stored on a hard disk. Network performance also can be influenced by the hard disk access time; a disk accessed in 15 milliseconds provides faster service than one that is accessed in 60 milliseconds. Since accessing files on the hard disk is a major activity for the file server, disk access time is important.

Hard Disks

Consider buying a hard disk with large storage capacity; 300MB may seem like a great deal, but may be a minimum needed depending on the number of programs and the size of the databases to be installed. Libraries typically do not provide storage space for user files because these files could quickly consume hard disk space. However, some software, such as WordPerfect and Microsoft Word, may require temporary hard disk space to operate. It is best to purchase the biggest and fastest drives possible. If a large capacity hard disk cannot be purchased immediately, then the file server should have the capability of adding hard disks later.

Backup Systems

A tape backup system is a useful component of the LAN. It provides a faster, and sometimes automatic, means of backing up the file server hard disk. A system that can be set to back up files automatically at a scheduled time is convenient because it allows backups to occur after the library is closed and when the LAN is not in use. Hard disks at individual stations also can be backed up with tape backup systems using LAN utility programs, such as Map Assist for Novell LANs.

Power Supply

As with any hard disk, the file server's hard disk can be damaged during sudden power outages and power surges. An uninterruptible power supply can protect against changes in power level and provide temporary electrical power when needed. Some LANs support uninterruptible power supplies that can automatically close down the server in event of power failure so that the files cannot be damaged and the integrity of the LAN is maintained. The uninterruptible power supply does not protect the individual workstations, but it does protect the most crucial and most expensive component of the LAN, its file server.

Workstations

Typically, the workstation can be any standard microcomputer compatible with the LAN. Additional RAM may be important for individual workstations since the LAN software and DOS all consume RAM. Add-on software, like menus, E-mail, or other utilities, also often require RAM. Some application software, such as WordPerfect and Lotus 1-2-3, requires more than 300K RAM and may not work if sufficient RAM is not available. The amount of RAM needed on a workstation depends upon the LAN software, the application software, and the type of workstation. Hard disks are not essential for public access microcomputers that will serve as LAN workstations since the file server can provide hard disk access. However, hard disks at individual workstations can be used to distribute software that is not available on the LAN or for software that needs to reside on a local hard disk.

In most LANs, the file server primarily distributes software that is then processed locally at each workstation. The file server may run at 25 MHz, but the local workstation may process software at only 8 or 12 MHz. In most instances, this discrepancy is not problematic. But in situations where users will perform extensive database management manipulation or elaborate mathematical calculations, local workstations may need to be more powerful.

The ability to run software with certain specifications remains dependent upon the capability of the local workstation; for example, color graphics, math coprocessors, and other features must be available at the local station, and are not necessary for the file server.

Some LANs can support stations that automatically start up the LAN when the microcomputer is turned on. A *boot ROM chip* installed on the network board in the station provides this capability and eliminates the need for start-up disks that must be circulated and can be damaged or misplaced. Boot ROM chips are unnecessary for workstations with hard disks since the AUTOEXEC.BAT files on the hard disk can be modified to include the network log-in steps. Boot ROM chips may not work in LANs connected to an institution's wide area network.

Wiring

Wiring configurations differ depending upon the LAN chosen. Wiring is subject to limitations (maximum cable length, maximum number of stations on any one leg of the LAN, for example) and specific configurations (such as bus, star, and token ring). Network wiring is different from electrical wiring and should be designed and installed by someone with LAN experience. Since the wiring provides the means for the workstations and file servers to communicate, it must be installed carefully and correctly. In some LAN wiring configurations, one weak link can disrupt the entire LAN.

Some situations make wiring easier to install. The building may have telephone wiring that can be used for the LAN. If a LAN is confined to a single room, wiring may simply involve *daisy-chaining* the stations together. See figure 5.1.

SOFTWARE ISSUES

There are two types of software involved in a LAN:
- the network software that runs the LAN itself
- the application software (programs for word processing, computer-based instruction, and other functions)

Network software may take many hours, even weeks, to learn. Understanding the general features of network software is an important basis for designing the LAN. These include
- establishing users and groups
- assigning rights for different users
- assigning shareable files

Figure 5.1. Local Area Network Configuration

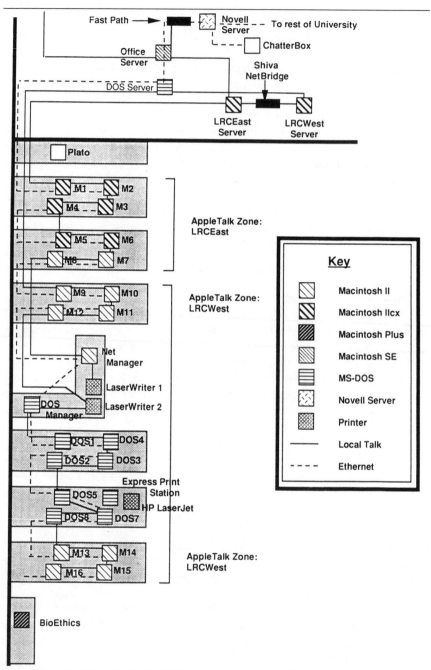

(Uniformed Services University of the Health Sciences, Learning Resource Center, used with permission)

- maintaining security
- establishing start-up specifications
- establishing shared peripherals
- establishing other special features

Establishing the LAN can be a very time-consuming process. Libraries may find consultant assistance valuable, although it is important to develop on-site expertise in using the LAN software for ongoing operations and maintenance.

Users and Use

Public access facilities can have a large number of potential users, so consider carefully how LAN users and levels of access are defined. Some libraries create a general default access level by assigning a network user name to each workstation that is available to any library user. Other libraries assign individual names to each user; this requires more effort in establishing network users, but it also provides more control over who can use the LAN and which files different users can access.

Other user access issues to consider are whether to provide user space on the file server hard disk on either a temporary or permanent basis; whether to limit user access to only certain DOS or other operating system commands in order to restrict potential user modification of files; whether, and how, to provide for use of software brought in by individuals.

Software Installation

Installing most software onto a LAN is usually only a little more difficult than installing software onto a hard disk. Most application software seems to operate routinely on LANs, although some problems may occur when software is shared by multiple, simultaneous users. Some software programs, such as WordPerfect, have special network versions or are especially designed to function on LANs. Inquire about the availability of network versions when purchasing software.

LANs provide the technology for an almost limitless number of users to share software simultaneously. However, copyright and software license agreements prevail over the technology. In order to provide application software on a shared basis, libraries need to secure network license agreements from the software publishers. These agreements may prohibit the library from installing the software on a LAN, even if only one user is allowed access at any given time. Some software publishers require libraries to purchase sufficient copies or site licenses for the maximum number of simultaneous users. Other publishers require licenses for every station on the LAN, sometimes making networked use of the software prohibitively expensive. Still other publishers have very reasonable special pricing and license agreements for LANs. These licenses will cost much more than a single copy, but should enable more users to access the software.

LANs can designate software as nonshareable, allowing only one use at a time. Some LANs have software metering utilities, such as LANShell and Saber Meter for Novell NetWare, that "count out" the licensed number of copies so that only a defined number of users can access the software at any one time.

Although not a major problem, some software developed under other operating systems, like the newer OS/2 or the older *UCSD-p System*, may not work on a DOS-based LAN. Other software may not be able to be installed on a LAN due to legal or operational constraints. It is necessary to make alternate arrangements for the distribution of these non-LAN programs and for the circulation of manuals for LAN-based software. Libraries may need two systems for distributing software: the LAN for software for which the library has the necessary copies or license agreements, and another system to accommodate the circulation of disks for software that is too expensive or not feasible to support through a LAN.

MAINTAINING A LAN

Maintaining a fully operational LAN is not as time consuming as the efforts to establish the LAN, but it still requires a significant amount of time. One of the most important routine maintenance tasks is backing up the files on the file server. For LANs providing access to databases or storing other data files, daily backup of the file server is essential. Some LANs store data onto two hard disks so that a backup is created continually. For LANs that are primarily used to distribute software and do not have files or programs on the hard disk that change often, backups can be made less frequently—weekly or after every software addition or revision. Several tape cartridges or disks should be available for making backups, so they can be used on a rotating basis and so that some copies can be archived to be replaced monthly or yearly. Multiple, staged backup copies are useful to protect against computer viruses or other damage. If the most recent backup is not usable, then an earlier backup may be helpful, even if it is not the most current copy.

Other LAN maintenance tasks include
- installing new application software
- creating new and deleting old user assignments
- providing LAN training for new users
- troubleshooting hardware and software problems
- monitoring usage and network performance
- adding new LAN stations
- upgrading LAN software when new versions are developed
- establishing new features such as remote access to the LAN or wide area network communications
- tracking developments in the LAN industry to identify solutions to problems and enhancements to the network

COSTS

Figure 5.2 shows approximate costs, in 1989, involved in establishing a LAN in both the MS-DOS and Macintosh environments. Costs for the individual workstations are not included, but can be derived from information provided in Chapter Three (Planning Facilities). Include a network board for each MS-DOS workstation. Wiring costs have not been included. A Macintosh LAN using Localtalk wiring would have minimal costs if the stations were clustered together. A LAN with stations dispersed throughout the library would have much higher wiring costs.

Figure 5.2 Approximate Costs of LANs

	MS-DOS	Macintosh
File server	$ 8,000	$6,000
Network board	400	
Wiring		
Tape backup	2,500	2,500
Uninterruptible power supply	450	450
Network software	4,500	800
TOTAL	$15,850	$9,750

SUMMARY

Local area networks have many advantages but they do require a more sophisticated level of technical expertise to install and maintain. Managing a LAN requires a significant time commitment and perhaps additional staff. The decision to establish a LAN involves weighing the advantages and disadvantages for the individual library.

Further Reading

Durr M, Gibson M. Networking personal computers. 3d ed. Carmel, IN:Que, 1989.
Madron TW. Local area networks: the second generation. New York:Wiley, 1988.
Veljkov MD. MacLans: local area networking with the Macintosh. Glenview, IL: Scott Foresman, 1988.

Chapter Six
Software Collections

This chapter covers various aspects of software collections including
- software types and sources
- collection development issues
- purchasing software
- preparation of software for use
- bibliographic control and circulation of software

We have not attempted to provide an exhaustive list of software relevant to health sciences libraries, but rather have identified sources for software. Information about software for hard disk security is included in Chapter Four (Equipment and Peripherals).

SOFTWARE TYPES AND SOURCES

Unfortunately, there is no *Books in Print* for microcomputer software. There are many directories and catalogs, but no single source covers all software or even that subset of educational software useful for students in the health professions. Librarians will need to refer to a variety of selection tools including online databases (AVLINE, SOFT, and Computer Database), directories, journals, electronic bulletin boards, and catalogs such as those listed at the end of this chapter. Other health sciences libraries' software collections can also be useful selection tools since many programs are developed locally and publicized only by word-of-mouth.

Major categories of software for use in health sciences public access microcomputer facilities and sources for identifying these types of programs are discussed here.

Educational Software

Educational software can be in the form of tutorials that present instructional material, quizzes that test knowledge, and simulations that mimic real situations. Educational software programs appropriate to the health sciences can generally be divided into (1) those for practitioners and (2) those for students. Educational software for patients is also available, but is not covered in this book.

Continuing education software, primarily intended for practitioners, is often very useful to students as well, especially those in the clinical years of instruction. Continuing education software for physicians usually is available from commercial software publishers who work in cooperation with content experts. A few examples include Cyberlog from Cardinal Health Systems, DiscoTest from Scientific American Medicine, the RxDx series from Williams & Wilkins, and the Cardiac Arrest Simulation Program from Aspen Systems. This type of program is widely advertised and reviewed in such journals as *JAMA, The New England Journal of Medicine,* and *MD Computing.* Librarians usually receive advertisements about such programs or get recommendations for purchase from physicians who have received advertisements.

Educational software for health sciences students is often more difficult to identify. Faculty in many different institutions have developed software for use in specific courses, either on their own or in cooperation with commercial distributors. These programs are advertised and distributed in a variety of ways. The easiest to identify are published and distributed through commercial sources such as Biosoft, the Health Sciences Consortium, and JB Lippincott. Pharmaceutical companies, such as the Upjohn Company and Merck, Sharp, & Dohme, have developed and distributed educational software. Other distribution sources for faculty-developed software include Academic Courseware Exchange (previously distributed by Kinko's and now Intellimation), Wisc-Ware, and the Chariot Software Group.

Other educational software is more difficult to identify. Faculty have started their own businesses to distribute software, for example, Minnesota Medical Edu-Ware distributes MacPharmacology, Command Applied Technology distributes Cardiovascular Systems and Dynamics and other software, and Roy Peterson distributes MacBaby (Fundamentals of Human Embryology) and other software. Some universities distribute software, including the University of Colorado's Biomedical Communications and the University of Missouri, Kansas City, School of Medicine. Advertising for this type of software may be minimal. As a result, the identification of high quality noncommercial software can be a serendipitous process.

Contacts with other academic health sciences librarians are very important in identifying locally created software. Other sources of information are professional conferences for (1) librarians, for example, meetings of the Health Sciences Communications Association and the Medical Library Association; (2) educators, for example, meetings of the Association of American Medical Colleges and the Association of American Dental Colleges; (3) researchers and clinicians, for example, Federation of American Societies for Experimental Biology and the American Academy of Otolaryngology; and (4) academic and medical computing professionals, for example, EDUCOM, the American Medical Informatics Association (which combines AAMSI, ACMI, and SCAMC), the IBM Academic Computing Conference, and the University of Tennessee's Information Technology in the Health Sciences Conference. Information comes both from colleagues who have software collections and from presentations or exhibits describing new software developments and products. Preliminary programs and conference proceedings provide useful information when attendance is not possible.

CD-ROM Products

There are an increasing number of CD-ROM products that are useful in public access facilities. MEDLINE on CD-ROM is probably the primary one offered in health sciences libraries. However, many other CD-ROM resources may be of interest, including (1) other bibliographic databases such as the Cumulated Index to Nursing & Allied Health Literature and Science Citation Index; (2) nonbibliographic databases such as DNASIS and PROSIS, DNA and protein sequencing tools; (3) reference sources such as Books in Print, Microsoft Bookshelf, and the American Society of Hospital Pharmacists' Drug Information Source, the PDR on CD-ROM; and (4) electronic textbooks such as Scientific American Medicine's Consult. Exhibits at library conferences such as the annual meetings of the Medical Library Association, the American Library Association, and ONLINE provide demonstrations of many different CD-ROM products appropriate for health sciences library users. Journals and directories such as *CD-ROM Librarian* and *The LaserDisk Professional* are also useful selection sources. Researchers may be valuable sources for information about scientifically oriented CD-ROM products.

Clinical Decision Aids and Practice Management Software

Decision-support software, office- and patient-management programs, and other tools useful for the practice of medicine are often very expensive and of greater value in clinical settings than in libraries. However, some of this software may be used in teaching or to acquaint users with its availability. These primarily commercial packages are listed in directories, such as *DataSources* and *Datapro Directory of Microcomputer Software;* in journals, such as *MD Computing;* and are exhibited at conferences for health professionals.

Computer Literacy Software

Educational software that teaches people how to use microcomputers and specific software programs can complement other efforts to encourage computer literacy. It may be necessary to acquire some of these programs to provide training opportunities that do not rely on staff assistance. Some of these programs, such as those by FlipTrack, include audiocassettes with a disk of practice files; others, such as those by Cdex-Intellisance, allow the user to run the software being learned along with the tutorial software so that help can be "requested" as needed. This type of software can be identified through catalogs and directories. User groups may be another source of identification and recommendation.

Productivity Software

Productivity software enhances one's ability to get a task done and includes applications such as word processing, database management, spreadsheet, reprint file management, statistical analysis, communications, and graphics programs. Many of these applications are commonly used throughout an institution, and one should follow the accepted institutional standards for purchase whenever possible. Institutions may have special site licenses or volume discount agreements with software publishers for certain programs.

Since productivity software is among the most popular software sold, there are many sources for purchase, including discount software stores and mail-order companies. Information is readily available in directories, catalogs, and computer magazines like *PC Magazine*, *MacUser*, and many others. Public domain and *shareware* software may provide satisfactory alternatives to commercially available productivity software. The various product-oriented online databases are also useful sources of information.[1]

COLLECTION DEVELOPMENT

There is a multitude of software packages from various sources. Some programs cost thousands of dollars and others are free. Since budgets are limited, a collection development policy for software purchase is useful. It is necessary to determine library goals in providing public access microcomputer facilities and to acquire software accordingly; see Chapter Two (Funding) for a more extensive discussion about library goals.

Collection development policies need to be formulated with the entire library service in mind. For example, word processing and other productivity software demand a higher level of service than educational software. Users will expect assistance with the software that is available to them. Knowledge of other easily accessible facilities and software in the institution may eliminate the need to duplicate those resources in the library.

Examples of library collection development goals include

- to provide computer-based instructional programs to support the clinical years of the medical school curriculum
- to provide a central facility for expensive resources needed by individuals on an occasional basis, such as interactive videodisc
- to provide productivity tools (for example, word processing) to increase student computer literacy
- to provide a facility for evaluation of clinically oriented software
- to provide end users with access to computerized databases, either on-line or CD-ROM

The following is a sample collection development statement.

Example

LOUISE DARLING BIOMEDICAL LIBRARY
COLLECTION DEVELOPMENT POLICY FOR
COMPUTER SOFTWARE

Introduction

The mission of the Biomedical Library is to acquire and make available those intellectual materials that will aid its primary user groups in their pursuit of education, research, and patient care. Computer software encompasses various contents, but essentially is information stored in a format different from traditional ones.

To the degree that it supports the library's mission, computer software should be collected on the same basis as print and other nonprint information. However, the present relative newness of microcomputer use in the educational process, and the high cost of many software packages, mandates that the collection development policy for software can not be bound too strictly to that for conventionally published materials. At this time the Biomedical Library can not hope to approach the level of coverage that it achieves for print materials within scope; buying of software will have to be selective. Committed as it is to service for its users, the Biomedical Library must also support computer literacy, and this may require buying software in areas that are beyond the usual Biomedical Library collection scope. More than in other areas of collection development, the microcomputer software resources of other campus units, as well as other library units, become relevant.

General considerations

This software collection development policy statement is intended to aid decisions on what software is acquired in support of the University's and the Biomedical Library's missions. It is not concerned with software for internal staff use, because decisions on acquisition of such programs will be made in other contexts.

Normal collection development criteria, such as applicability to user needs, Collection Review Committee judgment, faculty advice, opinions of the product expressed in reviews, reputation of the publisher/producer, etc., will be considered in this medium as in all others. In addition, such special criteria as ease of use of the program, its flexibility, the quality of accompanying documentation, and whether additional software is needed for its use, must be taken into consideration. Normally, software will be considered for purchase only if it can run on an IBM PC or XT, particularly on the configurations available in the Biomedical Library. If programs would necessitate purchase of different hardware, or a different operating system, their acquisition would have to be justified with the strongest possible reasons.

Normal collection development criteria will also apply as far as retention and weeding of the software collection. For example, some outdated teaching programs may be kept for historical documentation of the development of microcomputer education in the health sciences.

Examples of software classes to be acquired
1) courseware—instructional programs that will teach, illustrate, and drill (*CAI*); (highest priority)
2) applications programs—software written to perform a specific function; such programs include, but are not limited to:
   a) authoring programs—software designed for the creation of "expert" systems, or for the writing of new CAI programs;
   b) gateway programs—software designed to facilitate access to a variety of databases;
   c) bibliography programs—software designed to assist in the gathering, maintenance, and publication of bibliographies;
   d) practice management programs—for physicians', dentists', nurses' offices;
3) electronic publications
   a) numerical data files
   b) electronic journals
   c) books, reference works, etc.

Specific selection criteria
1) Courseware: selected on the same basis as are other instructional nonprint materials. Initiative to purchase will often originate from a faculty request, or from library awareness of curricular developments. We can not seek to cover comprehensively with computer courseware all health sciences classes, but will buy as heavily as necessary within the constraints of the acquisitions budget. If the LRD director (with input from other librarians) identifies significant and useful courseware he/she can buy it without faculty request, based upon the general selection criteria mentioned above.

2) Applications programs: those programs that are carried by the OAC Microcomputer Laboratory or other organized campus units will be bought very sparingly; interested users will be referred to these other locations when appropriate. For programs particularly appropriate for our primary user population, such as bibliographic access and organization software, we will buy to a fuller level; examples are programs for setting up personal information files, bibliography formatting, statistical packages, and database searching aids.

The Library will acquire selectively software designed to build *expert systems* that are useful for *writing CAI programs*. The Learning Resources Division and other staff will actively promote the use of such programs to design courseware specifically applicable to UCLA curricula. Such an approach will assure the existence of relevant teaching programs at minimal overall cost to the library. Faculty advice before purchase is especially necessary in this case, because ease of use and personal preference are particularly important with this type of program.

The Library will be highly selective in acquiring samples of programs which are designed to aid the physician, nurse, dentist, or allied health worker in their office or hospital *practice management*. Selection should be based mostly on software reviews in medical journals and on user recommendations.

3) Electronic publications: The area of *numerical data files* will demand close coordination between the Biomedical Library and the ISSR Data Archives, or any other organized collection including such materials that is accessible to the UCLA public. During this beginning stage of availability of data files on diskettes we can proceed conservatively. *Small* data sets, arranged in an accessible way and well indexed, might serve as appropriate introductions to this type of material. Any reasonable request by faculty for data within scope should be acquired. Experience will help to develop this policy further.

Electronic journal acquisition will be based on criteria applied to all journal decisions. For the near future, we will prefer to acquire the print format if both are available, unless use of the title is extremely sporadic and electronic access would be much cheaper. The same considerations hold true for *electronic books* or *reference works*.

(University of California, Los Angeles, Louise Darling Biomedical Library, used with permission)

Criteria for Selection

Once the overall goals are determined, specify the criteria for selecting which software to purchase. The relative importance of any one feature depends upon the software under consideration, its anticipated use, and the availability of alternatives. For example, there are many different MEDLINE CD-ROM products; one can review the features of several to select the best "fit" for the library. For other software, there may be less choice.

Audience or Intended User

Different software in the collection may be intended for different user populations. Some software packages intended for practicing professionals are also useful for advanced level students or residents; other packages, such as statistical analysis software, require considerable knowledge and extensive training. Librarians should have an idea, before making the purchase, who is likely to use that particular program. If library users and library staff will share access to the software or CD-ROM resources, suitability of the software for library staff should also be considered.

Ease of Use

Depending on the level of support provided to users, ease of use may be the highest priority for selecting software. This is especially true for productivity tools, such as word processing and some CD-ROM products, for which there are many programs with different features requiring different amounts of training.

Cost

Significant variations in price exist. Interactive video and CD-ROM products are more expensive than computer-based educational software programs, which usually cost less than commercial productivity tools. Shareware and public domain software may be the primary source of software if budgets are minimal.

Accuracy of Information Presented

For educational software and clinical decision-making tools, accuracy of the information is a key criterion. Accuracy should be determined by content experts, such as a physician or the faculty who will be using the software. Determine the publisher's commitment to provide revised versions as information changes.

Ability to Get Preview Copies

Preview a copy of the software before purchase to determine its suitability. An important step is faculty evaluation of educational software to assure that it is appropriate for the local curriculum. Trial use of CD-ROM databases can help determine which product the users and librarians like best. Previewing software is possible in most cases either with demonstration disks (sometimes free, sometimes for a fee) or on approval. Demonstration programs often display the end results of programs rather than how they work. It is not unreasonable to make preview of the complete program a condition of the sale, although some producers will not agree to these terms. Software stores often provide facilities for previewing commercially available software, as do many universities. Also, software reviews in journals may provide sufficient information to make a purchase decision.

Standards

When institutional standards—either stated or implicit—exist, library purchases should support them. This promotes consistency throughout the institution, and also means that users
- may already be familiar with the programs
- may require less assistance
- will have more sources of assistance when it is needed
- can exchange files with other people within the institution

When no institutional standard exists, selection of the prevailing market leader for any particular application is usually a good choice.

Developing library standards also is a good idea. For example, if multiple CD-ROM databases are available for users, a consistent interface from the same vendor is useful. Decide which databases will be offered and determine their availability from a single vendor.

Ability to Make Backup Copies

Backup copies are essential in a library where software is used by many different people and can be easily damaged. Some publishers permit the creation of a working copy. Other software is copy-protected so that if the disk becomes damaged a new one must be obtained. Some publishers sell backup copies for an additional fee at the time of purchase; others require evidence of a damaged disk, leading to a time delay in replacement. Some copy-protected software cannot be used on a hard disk.

Licensing Agreement Restrictions

Software publishers are primarily interested in prohibiting software buyers from making multiple copies, but license agreements may include other restrictions and should be scrutinized to assure that the library can agree to the terms before purchase. Special license agreements are required for using software on local area networks.

Compatibility with Available Equipment

Check operating requirements carefully. Many of the productivity programs can be installed to work with different equipment configurations, but educational software, especially interactive video, often has very specific requirements.

Equipment requirements are important criteria for selecting CD-ROM products. Libraries may prefer a multiple stack of CD-ROM drives to allow multiyear searching of the MEDLINE database without changing CD-ROM disks. Others may prefer several single CD-ROM drives attached to different workstations to provide simultaneous access by more users.

Diversity vs. User Support

Users may want the library software collection to include several different word processing programs or other productivity tools to accommodate individual preferences. Librarians need to weigh that service against the ability of library staff to support many different programs. User support issues may require librarians to select only one software program for each productivity area.

Multiple Copies

Librarians may want to use their budgets to buy different titles rather than multiple copies of the same title. Use may demand multiple copies for word processing or software that has been assigned by an instructor. Investigate volume purchase discounts or LAN versions if networks are used.

Version Updates

Some software programs undergo frequent updates and revisions resulting in continual expense to the library. Usually, only major version changes are important. However, upgrading from one version to the next may be fairly inexpensive, while upgrades for software that has had several version changes may be costly. Libraries should weigh the advantages of the new version against the cost to upgrade the software. Also, there are usually fewer compatibility problems with files created by different versions when the versions are closer together.

PURCHASING SOFTWARE

Purchasing educational software is straightforward since there is usually only one distributor for each program. When purchasing productivity tools, librarians should shop around for the lowest price. Special discounts are available to educational institutions. Some software publishers, like Microsoft, WordPerfect, and Claris, handle educational sales directly; other publishers, like MicroPro and Borland International, use distributors such as Chambers International (Boca Raton, FL) and Campus Technology Products (Leesburg, VA) to provide educational discounts. Local software stores in competition with each other may be willing to negotiate lower prices. Mail-order businesses may offer low price alternatives.

Publishers and distributors may offer discounts for multiple copies of software. Some require purchase of one full package and then sell licenses to use the software on additional workstations at a small price per station. Others sell multiple copies of the full package at discounts dependent upon the number of copies purchased. Special package deals are available for local area networks, such as licenses to use the software at five workstations for the price of one. Although a time-consuming process, exploring options for purchasing software probably will result in obtaining lower prices.

Budgetary Considerations

Software budgets differ depending on the library, the library's goals in providing public access microcomputer facilities, the priority of the microcomputer facility among other library services, and the number of workstations for which software must be provided. Some medical libraries with public access facilities have software budgets of less than $2,000, while others have more than $20,000. Libraries with media facilities often combine the computer software budget with the media program budget, providing more flexibility in spending within a specific year. In larger libraries, funding for software may come from various accounts. CD-ROM products may be purchased from budgets for reference tools or online services, while educational software is purchased with media acquisitions funds. A stable software budget ensures the ability to purchase new software as it appears and to update older versions. Special annual gifts or grants may be a good way of financing subscription renewals for software like Cyberlog and DiscoTest, which otherwise could consume a significant portion of the annual budget.

To establish a software budget, identify examples of programs that would be purchased each year from the sources listed at the end of this chapter, and determine prices and the quantities to be purchased. Librarians with similar facilities also can provide an indication of software budget needs.

Compliance with Copyright

The copyright law, 17 U.S.C. Section 117, allows the library to make a backup copy for archival purposes. However, most software programs are licensed rather than sold, and those license agreements rather than the copyright law govern the way libraries can use a specific software package. Often, licensing conditions are included on the packaging; opening the package implies agreement to the terms. As a possible means of protection, some libraries are including a statement on the order form indicating to the software distributor, before purchase, the intended use.

Example of information provided on purchase orders
PURCHASE IS ORDERED FOR LIBRARY CIRCULATION AND
PATRON USE.
VENDOR ACCEPTANCE OF THIS ORDER ACKNOWLEDGES
BUYER'S RIGHT TO MAKE A BACKUP COPY OF NON-COPY-
PROTECTED SOFTWARE OR TO RECEIVE SHIPMENT OF VENDOR
PROVIDED BACKUP COPY IF COPY PROTECTED.

(University of California, Irvine, Biomedical Library, Serials/Acquisitions Department, used with permission)

Just as libraries must notify users of the copyright laws governing photocopies, they also must inform users that software is copyrighted and should not be copied. Some libraries post copyright warning signs at the circulation desk or at each workstation. Others include electronic messages on the disks or through the local area network. Some libraries have users sign a statement indicating that the user will comply with copyright laws as a condition for using the microcomputer. Public access microcomputer facilities are a potential haven for software pirates; libraries are legally and ethically obligated to discourage illegal copying and to comply with copyright and license agreements.

Sample copyright statement
SOFTWARE IS PROTECTED BY COPYRIGHT, 17 U.S.C. SECTION
101. UNAUTHORIZED COPYING IS PROHIBITED BY LAW.[2]

PREPARING SOFTWARE FOR USE

Software requires considerably more processing effort than a book does before it is ready to use. The degree of effort depends on how the programs are made available to users (on floppy disks, on a hard disk, or through a local area network), how the program is packaged, whether or not the program is cataloged, and if the program requires installation for local use.

Installing and Testing Software

Always read instructions first and make backup copies of disks whenever possible before installing software. The original or backup copies should be placed in a secure storage area. Installation of the software may include configuring it for a specific printer or monitor, establishing defaults to disk drives and communications ports, and setting other defaults to personal preferences such as page format in word processing programs. Some programs, such as Grateful Med, come in a compact, archived format and must be converted into a standard format before use.

Loading software onto a hard disk or a local area network may be as easy as copying it from the floppy disk to the hard disk, or it may involve elaborate procedures described in the manuals accompanying the software. To make programs easier for users to start up, software circulated on disks should be *self-booting*, that is, include system start-up files on the disk, and self-starting, that is, include an AUTOEXEC.BAT file for DOS-formatted disks.

Test the software on the equipment available to make sure it operates properly. This is especially important with noncommercial educational software, which may have been developed for specific equipment only. For example, the early IBM PCs included *BASICA* in ROM whereas *BASIC* was disk-based in IBM PC-compatible computers. Programs written with the IBM BASICA would look for BASIC in ROM rather than on a floppy disk or hard disk. Programs written for one type of graphics monitor (monographic, CGA, EGA, or VGA) may not work properly on another. Testing the software also will identify damaged disks or improperly installed software before it is used.

Packaging Software

The effort required to package software depends upon how the software is stored and its original packaging. Regular library shelving works well for storing software collections. It is readily available, makes the software easily accessible, and is well suited for bulky manuals. Locked storage cabinets or file drawers are other alternatives for storing software.

Many software programs come in packaging that is suitable for shelving or filing, adequately protects the disks, and incorporates accompanying documentation. In other cases, libraries must repackage it. One effective,

Figure 6.1. Examples of Packaging Techniques

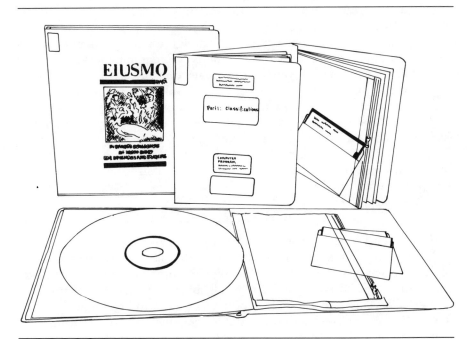

secure storage device for disks is an 8″ by 10.5″ (or smaller for 3.5″ disks) three-hole-punched, plastic pocket with a zipper (sold in stationery stores). It can be placed in a three-ring binder along with any loose sheets of documentation. Soft-cover manuals can be bound to prolong wear. Interactive videodisc programs can be packaged in plastic jackets designed for circulating phonograph records; these are available through library supplies catalogs. Accompanying documentation and disks can be placed inside the sleeves or in a plastic zip pocket affixed to the sleeve. See figure 6.1.

Software package labels should conform with other library materials. Disks and other parts should be labeled individually in case they become separated from the package. Libraries with theft detection systems should check with the system manufacturer about ways to prevent theft of computer disks. One academic library uses 3M Tattle Tape theft detection strips on 5.25″ disks, hiding them under labels. The information on the disks maintains its integrity as long as the disk is not demagnetized with the activator/deactivator device. Manuals should also be protected; manuals for popular software are prime targets of theft.

Instructions for Users

If software is available by more than one means—on workstations with hard disks, through the local area network, or as disks circulated through a reserve desk—users need to know where to find the software in order to use it. Libraries can provide information about software location and access in handouts, lists, or cataloging information.

In libraries with different equipment configurations, users must know which equipment to use for which programs. The equipment requirements can be given with the software and manuals, on software lists, in cataloging information, or all of the above. For example, a note on the software package label might read: "This program requires color graphics and a math coprocessor." Instructions for how to start up the program should be included with the software, even if they are as simple as "Place disk in Drive A and turn on computer." This assumes, of course, that the user knows where to find Drive A, or that additional instructions for using the equipment are provided.

BIBLIOGRAPHIC CONTROL

Users need to know what software the library has and where to find it. Computer software should be treated like other library materials and cataloged according to standard AACR2 rules. Records for software should be included in the library's catalog so that all library materials are identified in one source. This is especially helpful to users who are interested in a specific topic regardless of the format. On the other hand, many users may want to know only about the software available in the library. Be prepared to meet this need as well, whether through a heading in the main catalog that clusters software or on a separate list.

Lists of software can be adequate alternatives if cataloging is not possible or practical. These lists should give users sufficient information to be able to identify suitable items. This includes title, equipment requirements (for example, MS-DOS computer, Macintosh computer), publisher, date, version number, and identification number or location (for example, call number, accession number, "on station 2," "on the network"). A short description also is very helpful. Lists of software become cumbersome to create and use when software collections expand beyond 100 titles. Lists created with database management software allow for greater flexibility in generating list subsets such as all Macintosh software, all educational software, or arrangements by title or call number. The database itself could be available for users to search. It could also be used to document information for administrative use such as software serial numbers, licensing stipulations, number of copies.

Example of software listings
  CARDIOVASCULAR SYSTEMS AND DYNAMICS
    1 disk (IBM PC) and manual
    Media WG 202 C2695 1985
    Pullman, WA: Command Applied Technology, 1985
    Simulates a pulsatile cardiovascular system and components.

HEARTLAB
1 disk (Macintosh), 1 sound interface module, and 1 manual
Media WG 141.5 A9 H436 1988
Boston, MA: Harvard Medical School, Dept. of Radiology, Brigham
& Women's Hospital, 1988
An interactive audio program simulating heart sounds. Auscultation
skills are honed in the laboratory mode while opportunity for mak-
ing diagnosis is available in the patient mode.
THE SUICIDAL ADOLESCENT: IDENTIFICATION, RISK
ASSESSMENT AND INTERVENTION
2 disks (IBM PC), 2 videodiscs (Pioneer LDV 6000 series videodisc
player)
Media HV 6546 S947 1987
Capitol Heights, MD: National Audiovisual Center, 1987
Designed to make physicians aware of the problems of adolescent
suicide. Helps users recognize the signs and symptoms of teenage
depression, assess risk factors, and determine appropriate intervention.

(University of Southern California, Norris Medical Library, used with permission)

Cataloging software is more time consuming than cataloging books since
(1) locating the title and other information requires running the program;
(2) less cataloging copy is available through AVLINE, OCLC, RLIN, or
other sources; and (3) more cataloging details such as format or system
requirements may be required. Libraries deal with these problems in different ways. In one academic medical library, the media/computer librarian
is responsible for cataloging the programs; in another, the microcomputer
facility staff installs the program and provides cataloging information to
the cataloger. In another library, the microcomputer facility staff prepares
the software and provides it to users, but sends the original disks to the
cataloging office for cataloging.

Cataloging Hints

• Title
  Whenever possible, title information should come from the software
  itself, not the accompanying manuals, packaging, or brochures. Often
  the opening screen contains the "title page" information. Indicate the
  source of the title information.
• System requirements
  System requirements (for example, 640K RAM required, runs on Macintosh SE and II, math coprocessor required) should include not only
  what equipment is available in the library but the general require-

ments for the software. Many of these requirements must be found in the accompanying manuals since some information, such as RAM requirements, cannot be determined from any other source.

- Number of disks
  The number of disks should include the original number that came with the software, not just those that are available for use. For example, word processing software may include installation utilities that would not be needed once the software is prepared for users.
- Version numbers
  These should be treated like different editions.

SOFTWARE CIRCULATION

When software is made available through hard disks or local area networks, circulation is primarily determined by policies governing use of the equipment. Who is authorized to use the equipment and for how long determine the "circulation," or use, of the software. When software is circulated on disks, libraries need policies and procedures regarding

- authorized users (students, faculty, clinicians)
- borrowing period (one hour, two hours, one day, renewals)
- use outside the library (for specific users, for specific software)
- reservations (required, optional, length of time, limits per day or week)
- determination of lost or damaged software (who checks, how frequently: after each use, daily)
- who circulates software (regular library circulation staff, special consultants)
- notification of copyright laws governing software (signed user statements, posted signs, labels on software)

SUMMARY

Software collection development goes hand-in-hand with equipment purchase to ensure the compatibility of equipment and software. Software collections are evidence of the library's commitment to provide microcomputer resources and support their use whether for education, information retrieval and management, or word processing. As with other library materials, selection and acquisition are the beginning steps; unlike books, which usually come ready to shelve, software often requires installation, repackaging, and modification to make it more "user friendly."

References
1. O'Leary M. Computer databases: a survey. Part 3: Product databases. Database, Apr 1987; 10(2):56–64.
2. Reed MH, Stanek D. Library and classroom use of copyrighted videotapes and computer software. Library Software Review, May–Jun 1986;5(3):160.

Software Catalogs, Databases, Directories, and Bulletin Boards

Academic Courseware Exchange
(formerly Kinko's)
Intellimation
130 Cremona Drive
P.O. Box 1922
Santa Barbara, CA 93116
(800)346-8355

Alternatives in Medical Education:
Non-Animal Methods
Physicians Committee for
Responsible Medicine
P.O. Box 6322
Washington, DC 20015

AAMSI Software Exchange
American Association for
Medical Systems and
Information
1101 Connecticut Avenue, NW,
Suite 700
Washington, DC 20036

Applelink
Apple Computer, Inc.
20525 Mariani Avenue
Cupertino, CA 95014

AVLINE
MEDLARS Management Section,
National Library of Medicine
8600 Rockville Pike
Bethesda, MD 20894

Hypercard Public Domain
Directory: Higher Education,
1988
Berkeley Macintosh Users Group
1442A Walnut Street, #62
Berkeley, CA 94709
(415)549-2684

Bolwell C. Directory of Educational
Software for Nursing. New
York:National League for
Nursing, 1988.

Cook V, McCorkel J. Computer-
assisted instruction for medicine
and nursing: sources and
programs. Bull Med Libr Assoc
1987 Apr;75(2):101–08.

Datapro Directory of
Microcomputer Software.
Delran, NJ:Datapro Research,
1981–.

DataSources: the Guide to
Computer Hardware, Software,
and Communications
Products—the Entire
Marketplace. New York:
Ziff-Davis, 1981–.

Directory of Software in Higher
Education. Compiled from the
Chronicle of Higher Education
OCLC Online Computer Library
Center, Inc.
6565 Frantz Road
Dublin, OH 43017

Directory of Software Sources for
Higher Education: A Resource
Guide for Instructional
Applications. Princeton, NJ:
Peterson's Guides, 1987.

Education Sector Software Catalog
Chambers International
Corporation, Education Industry
Marketing Group
5499 North Federal Highway,
Suite A
Boca Raton, FL 33487
(305) 997-9444

Educomp's Macintosh Public
Domain Software Catalog
2429 Oxford Street
Cardiff by the Sea, CA 92007

IBM MultiMedia Courseware
Pocket Guide
Ronda Rattray, IBM MultiMedia
Solutions
P.O. Box 2150
Atlanta, GA 30055
(404) 238-5676

Interactive Video: A Directory of
Users, Vendors, Producers,
Researchers, and Observers
Concerned with Interactive
Videodiscs and Related Optical
Technology, August 1987.
Applied Video Technology
5118 Westminster Place
St. Louis, MO 13108

Isaac (Information System for
Advanced Academic
Computing)
Isaac@uwaee or
M/S FC-06, University of
Washington
Seattle, WA 98195

MacGuide
The Delta Group, Inc.
818 17th Street, Suite 210
Denver, CO 80202
(303)825-8166

Macintosh Buyer's Guide
Redgate Communications Corp.
3381 Ocean Drive
Vero Beach, FL 32963
(305)231-6904

MDR Videodisc Consortium
Catalog
Stewart Publishing
6471 Merritt Court
Alexandria, VA 22312

Nursing Educator's MicroWorld
CAI Resource Book.
Saratoga, CA:Diskovery
Computer Assisted Healthcare
Education, 1989.

PC-SIG Encyclopedia of Shareware.
A comprehensive guide to low
cost software for IBM and compatibles. 5th Ed. Sunnyvale, CA:
PC-SIG, 1989.

Software and High Technology
Products for Higher Education
Campus Technology
Products Co.
15 Loudoun Street, SW
P.O. Box 2909
Leesburg, VA 22075
(703) 777-9110

Software Catalog: Microcomputers.
New York:Elsevier, 1983–.

Software Digest
Macintosh Ratings Report
One Winding Drive
Philadelphia, PA 19131
(800)223-7093

Software Encyclopedia. New
York:R.R. Bowker, 1985–.

Software for Health Sciences
Education: An Interactive
Resource. 2d Ed., 1989.
Learning Resource Center,
Office of Educational Resources
and Research
University of Michigan Medical
Center
1135 East Catherine Street
Ann Arbor, MI 48109
(313)763-6770

Wisc-Ware
  Academic Computing Center
  University of Wisconsin
  210 West Dayton Street
  Madison, WI 53706
  (608)262-8167

Journals

The Chronicle of Higher Education
  Contains software sources in
  Computer Column

JAMA
  Contains occasional reviews
  with book review section

M.D. Computing
  July issue includes: A Directory
  of Medical Software Companies.
  November issue includes:
  Buyer's Guide

*Medical Software Consortium
  Newsletter*
  Medical Software Consortium
  P.O. Box 76069
  St. Peters, MO 63376

*Medical Interactive Video Consortium
  Newsletter*
  Cindy Freeman, USUSH, Center
  for Interactive Media in
  Medicine
  4301 Jones Bridge Road
  Bethesda, MD 20814
  (202)295-6263

New England Journal of Medicine
  Contains occasional reviews
  with book review section

Wheels for the Mind
  Apple Computer, Inc.
  P.O. Box 1834
  Escondido, CA 92025

Further Reading

Gorman M, Winkler P, eds. Anglo-American cataloging rules. 2d ed., chapter 9:
  computer files. Chicago:American Library Association, 1988.
Olsen NB. Cataloging microcomputer software: a manual to accompany AACR2,
  chapter 9, computer files. Englewood, CO:Libraries Unlimited, 1988.
Woodsmall R, Lyon-Hartmann B, Siegel E. MEDLINE on CD-ROM. Medford, NJ:
  Learned Information, 1989.

Chapter Seven
User Services

Introducing public access microcomputers into a library leads to the development of many associated services and expectations of service levels. Some services, including instructions on operating equipment, are necessary to make microcomputers available and useful at the most basic level. Other, more specialized, services create opportunities for the library to go beyond the role of merely providing space for equipment and access to a software collection. These services can include formal teaching and consultation by library staff, sale of computer supplies and software, and sponsorship of computer user groups. The presence of microcomputer resources leads users to expect certain minimum standards of service, such as the equipment kept in working order and on-site staff available to provide basic assistance.

This chapter
- defines basic services and standards
- discusses other, specialized services

The focus is on direct user services not covered elsewhere in this book. For information about specific services not covered here—distributing software through a local area network, for example—consult the appropriate chapter or the index. Chapter Eight (Personnel) discusses staffing and skills needed to provide services. Chapter Nine (Administrative Issues) takes a broader view of providing services and discusses issues such as fees, statistics, and security.

THE BASICS

Many basic services related to microcomputers are similar to those that support other library resources. For instance, the resource must be available to meet the need for which it was intended. For microcomputers, availability means maintaining the hardware and software in working order and developing access policies and procedures that encourage appropriate use. Availability also means telling users what resources are available and how to use them, and monitoring use to support decisions about the future allocation of space, budget, and staff. Each library will determine its basic services according to its environment, clientele, budget, staff, and goals. There is no set formula of what to do or how to do it, but with more libraries providing access to microcomputers, there are many examples of what has been done.

Basic services include
- information about what is available
- equipment and software that work
- instructions
- basic user assistance
- printing services

Information about What Is Available

Users and potential users need accurate information about even the most popular services. Basic information includes
- what kinds of computers and peripherals are available
- procedures: where to borrow software, how to get access to microcomputers, printers, and other equipment
- what software packages are available
- what databases are available and what years do they cover
- circulation policies: who can use what and for how long
- reservation policies: who can make reservations, how, and for how long
- hours of operation
- when and what assistance is available on-site
- charges for printing, supplies, etc.
- fines

Services and resources should be advertised to notify users of their availability. Once users are aware of library services, they need additional information about the library's specific policies and procedures. Fact sheets, tours, library newsletters, and signs are traditional ways to inform users; electronic bulletin boards and feature articles in computer center or school newsletters are other effective communications channels.

Following the notion that information is most effective at the time it is needed, one health sciences library provides users with a three-ring binder containing the key needed to turn on the microcomputer. The binder contains library policies and procedures for using the facility, instructions for using the microcomputer and local area network, a floor plan showing where the workstations are located, and instructions for using the laser printer.

The following are examples from library fact sheets.

Example

The Microcomputer Room is located on the sixth floor of the College of Nursing/Health Sciences Learning Center in Room 604J. This room is equipped with 6 IBM AT's. One of these micros, MED01, cannot be utilized by users since it acts as a server, that is, stores software and controls the network of micros. The other 5 micros (MED02, MED03, MED04, MED05, and MED06) can be utilized.

The microcomputers are to be used by U.K. Medical Center faculty, staff, and students for educational and personal use. People from other departments of U.K. may use them on a space available basis.

(University of Kentucky Audio-Visual Library, College of Nursing/Health Sciences Learning Center, used with permission)

Example

The computers are for educational use by Health Sciences students and UM faculty and staff with current University IDs. Game playing is not permitted. Priority is given to students using programs on reserve for health sciences coursework although an effort will be made to keep at least one computer available for self-directed learning. When necessary, sign-up sheets will be posted in the computer carrels.

(University of Minnesota Bio-Medical Library Learning Resources Center, used with permission)

Equipment and Software that Work

Providing access to equipment implies a commitment to keeping that equipment in working order. A library might set as a service performance standard that a certain percentage of the equipment is ready to use at any time. Falling below the predetermined percentage would prompt action, such as a call to a repair service. Defective equipment should be labeled as "out of service" or removed from user areas. Repairs should be made promptly. Broken equipment is frustrating for users and gives a poor image to the facility.

Users should be encouraged to report, in detail, problems with the equipment. A preprinted form for describing equipment problems encourages users to inform staff and helps verify those problems. Good descriptions of what does not work can save time in diagnosis and repair.

Sample Form for Reporting Equipment Problems

WORKSTATION _____

PROBLEM _____

_____

_____

DATE _____

Regular preventive maintenance, such as keeping monitors clean, should be performed and is discussed in Chapter Four (Equipment and Peripherals).

Software also needs to be in good working condition with all of its parts (disks, manuals) intact. In an ideal situation, library staff should check software for defects and missing parts after each use. In reality, feedback from users may be the primary means of identifying problems. However, once a problem is identified, library staff should check the software to determine if the problem is user related or if a defect exists in the software. The problem should be dealt with promptly so that the software is out of circulation for only a short time.

Instructions

First-time use of most equipment requires some basic instruction. Finding the "on" switch for a computer device can be a frustrating challenge that is multiplied by the number of pieces of equipment involved. Although most software comes with instructions, additional and more basic instructions are often needed and appreciated. "Insert the DOS disk into the A drive" makes sense to the person who has done it before, but not necessarily to the novice user. Providing clear instructions for basic computer operation and software use serves both users and library staff since this information can reduce unnecessary dependence and demand on staff time.

The following sample forms can be adapted for different situations.

Example
Include with the software program.
Program Name: Writer

This word processing program requires at least 256 K of memory. To begin:

1. In order to save your work in this program, you need your own formatted disk in Drive B.
2. Insert Program Disk into Drive A.
3. Turn on computer; if it is already on, boot up system by pressing three keys simultaneously: CTRL, Alt, Del.
4. At the A > prompt, type WRITE.
5. To exit at any time, follow program instructions for saving your file and press the F3 key.

Note: Copyright law prohibits unauthorized use or copying of this software program.

Example
Post, in a protective covering, at a workstation.
Computer #3

This workstation includes
–an IBM computer with 640 K of memory
–two disk drives, labeled A and B
–an EGA color graphics monitor

This computer can be used with the library's local area network by typing in NET at the A> prompt. To get a printout of your work, you must first save it on your own formatted disk and take it to the printer in Room 202.

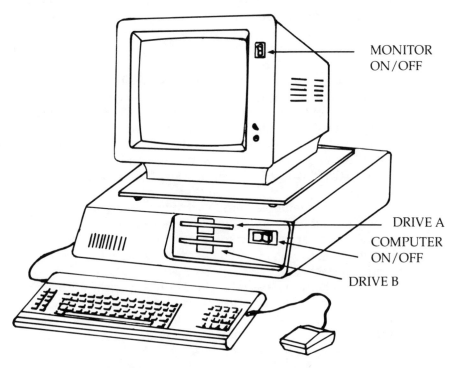

MONITOR
ON/OFF

DRIVE A
COMPUTER
ON/OFF
DRIVE B

Note: Copyright law prohibits unauthorized use or copying of most software programs.

The following is the text of a handout that provides hints for using word processing programs.

NO-Fuss Golden Rules of Word Processing

It has come to my attention recently that some common rules of basic word-processing are virtually unknown to many otherwise sophisticated medical school denizens. These will save you time and effort in the long run, even for a short document.

Rule #1: **Never ever ever** use returns at the end of a line of text that isn't the end of a paragraph. Doing so will cause you much misery and heartache when you have to delete them out of a thirty-page paper. The Mac is not a typewriter! When you reach the end of a line the computer will "word-wrap" where your right-hand margin has been placed. The right margin default is 6" which allows you to read your text on the Mac screen while you are working, but you can change it at any time, preferably before printing. Only put in a return when you mean it.

Rule #2: **Never ever ever** use spaces when what you really want is formatting. Use tabs, which you can create by clicking on your ruler (Word), or dragging one out of the "tab well" (Macwrite) and onto your ruler. The screen representation has little to do with how much space the words will actually take when you print. By using tabs you are telling the printer to align tabbed lines at 2", for example.

Rule #3: **Never ever ever** use tabs when what you really want is to move a segment of text over to the next line. If you do this, the next time you change the font, font size, or margins or change over to a different system (say for the Laserwriter) your perfectly lined up subheads will scoot back up to the next line or exhibit other nasty distortions. If you want a new line, hit Return, then move the left-hand margin as much as you need so that the new line lines up under the text in the way you want it.

OR, If you want multiple lines to wrap but be indented under a subhead or numbered paragraphs as I have demonstrated here, drag the indent arrow (Macwrite) to the right of the margin. In Word you drag the lower portion of the left margin triangle while holding down the shift key.

The opposite effect is easily obtained by dragging the top margin triangle in Word or the indent arrow in Macwrite to the right. This way you need not put 5 spaces every time you start a new paragraph or create a tab just for first line indenture, as is demonstrated in this paragraph's formatting.

Rule #4: If you don't understand some of the funny commands in the menus, exhibit some curiosity and try them out before they try you. Don't be afraid to look something up in the manual to figure out the best way to do it (page numbering, for example). In the long run, proper formatting will save you time and give you more editing flexibility. Doing it the wrong way may mean hours of cleaning up a formatting mess. If all else fails, ask for help.

(Stanford University Fleischmann Learning Resource Center, used with permission)

Basic User Assistance

Users will request assistance even if printed instructions are provided. There is a broad range of user assistance possible (including many specialized services described below); however, a basic level of assistance must be provided in all public access microcomputer environments.

At its most minimal level, assistance may be handing a user printed information in response to a question or providing a telephone and the number of a department that provides user assistance. At a higher level, basic assistance may include helping a user get the software started, format a disk, or perform other common microcomputer activities. The entire library staff may become involved, with different staff members helping based on their expertise and availability.

The use of computer-assisted instructional materials is usually fairly straightforward and requires minimal assistance. However, word processing, database management, statistical analysis, and similar programs can require extensive user support. Policies stating what type and how much assistance will be provided to whom should be set and advertised in advance. These policies can include time limits or restrictions on questions, for example, support limited to questions about software in the collection. Enforcing limits on user assistance is difficult and often best handled on a case-by-case basis within the context of a clearly defined policy. Written guidelines are invaluable as an objective recourse for the person being asked for help.

Example

The reference staff will be available to provide orientation on the basic use of the computers. Since each CAI program uses different commands, the patron will be responsible for reading the accompanying documentation to obtain complete instructions. If there is a problem with the equipment, the user is responsible for notifying the reference staff on duty in the LRC.

(National Library of Medicine Learning Resource Center, used with permission)

Good referral practices can extend user assistance services beyond the library. Local experts such as faculty, teaching assistants, computer center staff, and classes may be valuable referrals. Referral is discussed in more detail below, under "Specialized Services."

For example, in one library, three librarians and a library assistant help users turn on equipment and start up software; they provide more extensive assistance for software they themselves use. Other questions are referred to the medical center microcomputer consultant. People needing additional instruction about using software are referred to the courses offered by the medical center.

Printing Services

Most computer users expect to be able to print their work. Though users would like a laser printer at each workstation, few libraries can afford that. A dot-matrix printer may be attached to one or more computers; a laser printer may be available through a network. Printers require more attention than computers do (loading paper, clearing jams, changing ribbons) and involve the ongoing expense of paper and ribbons or cartridges. In some libraries, users are expected to supply their own paper; in other libraries, there is a charge for printing, either by the page or by the minute. Some libraries provide free dot-matrix printing, but charge for laser printing.

Libraries use a variety of mechanisms to charge for printing. Some use a self-service debit card or a coin-operated system that requires payment as each page is printed or after a certain amount of time has elapsed. Another option is a special printer service area with staff to assess and collect page fees. Some libraries use an honor system in which users pay the posted per-page fees. For a more detailed discussion of printers, see Chapter Four (Equipment and Peripherals); for a discussion about fees, see Chapter Nine (Administrative Issues).

SPECIALIZED SERVICES

Specialized services, which can be provided in association with public access microcomputers, may be directed to specific user populations, such as students or physicians, or may target everyone affiliated with the institution, including clerical and administrative staff. Services discussed in this section include
- information and referral
- formal user education programs
- consultation
- demonstration collections and equipment
- sale of supplies
- user groups

Information and Referral

Libraries have traditionally been places to go for information. Even a health sciences library without any microcomputers on-site can serve as a source of information about computer-related topics by
- subscribing to a few major computer journals, for example, *BYTE, PC Magazine,* and *MacUser*
- providing access to and promoting use of databases covering the computer literature such as the Microcomputer Index, the Microcomputer Software & Hardware Guide, and the Computer Database
- maintaining lists of computer equipment and systems available in the organization
- including equipment and software directories in reference collections
- maintaining files of relevant computer software reviews such as those in *JAMA*

Librarians have a long tradition of referral to authoritative resources. It makes sense to extend this tradition to microcomputer-related information. Directories and lists of software, equipment manufacturers, programming consultants, individuals within the institution working on computer projects, user groups, and courses can be useful resources if the referral files are kept current. Using a computer program to manage referral files, and perhaps making the files available through a computer network, are ways in which the library can be a recognized source for information that exists beyond the library itself.

Formal User Education Programs

Libraries can help people use computers and help support the computer-literacy efforts of parent institutions through a variety of instructional activities and products including
- individual instruction
- formalized group instruction
- self-instructional training materials, such as computer, video, or audio-cassette tutorials
- fact sheets that describe how to perform common operations, such as how to format a disk or copy files
- quick reference guides that get people started using software and performing basic functions

Users often want individual instruction when they need to use software, sometimes for help with an assignment due the next day. As mentioned above, library policy should define how much and what type of individual instruction will be provided. In one large academic health sciences library, health sciences instructors who give programming assignments schedule teaching assistants in the library specifically to help students in those courses.

Group instruction may seem like more effort but, in the long run, it may be more efficient than ad hoc individual assistance. Self-instructional materials, fact sheets, and quick reference guides also can answer many questions, thereby reducing demand on library staff time. Referral services, mentioned above, can also enhance user education efforts.

Some subjects and programs are of particular relevance to librarians' expertise including search systems software, such as Grateful Med, bibliographic reference management software, such as Pro-Cite, and modems and communications software, such as Smartcom and ProComm. Some health sciences librarians have gone beyond their more traditional areas of expertise to provide instruction on introductory microcomputer information and use of specific software programs for word processing, database management, and graphics. Many librarians are now involved in teaching computer-related credit courses in the health sciences schools.

Some libraries have been so successful in developing instructional programs that they serve as models or consultation resources for their institutions. While the reputation may benefit the library's image, the time spent teaching may be a drain on library staff resources. One option is to charge for classes and possibly open enrollment to the community; another option is for the library to act as a broker for training services provided by others.

Consultation

Consulting is a natural outgrowth of providing public access microcomputers. After people have received help in basic microcomputer operations from library staff, they are likely to ask for assistance or advice requiring more computer knowledge or software familiarity. They may even call for information and advice while working on their home or office computers. Consultation services increase the library's visibility. They can demonstrate the librarians' expertise in areas such as text management, database design, and information retrieval systems. As an added benefit, consulting also can educate librarians about information-related activities and needs outside of the library.

If provided, consultation should be a formalized library service with standards for degree of involvement (for example, will a staff member install programs?) and accountability for the quality of the advice given (what if someone buys a program on the recommendation of the library's consultant, and the program does not do what was expected?). Staffing for consultant services is discussed in Chapter Eight (Personnel). It is important to determine how consulting services relate to other support resources such as vendors, computer center staff, and faculty members. Decide how best to use the library's resources without duplicating services available elsewhere.

Decide if the service will be available to anyone who calls; if it is not, define how library staff will determine if the caller is eligible for the service. It may be possible to charge for some consulting services, such as programming assistance, or to work with other departments to provide the service. Since there are limits to the personal consulting assistance that can be provided, the library should provide referrals to other resources. Referral services are mentioned above, in the section "Information and Referral."

Demonstration Collections and Equipment

The library can also assist users in deciding what to purchase by providing examples of software and different types of equipment. Maintaining a collection of demonstration disks is one option, although most people agree that it is necessary to see an entire program to evaluate it properly. The library could serve as the institution's authorized representative for obtaining complete software packages for review. Vendors may provide free copies for this purpose. Some libraries have become their institution's source of public domain and shareware collections.

Equipment vendors could be approached about demonstrating the latest computer technology. The library can also serve as the location for testing and evaluating specialized equipment configurations and innovative programs such as those for interactive videodisc. Library staff members might solicit or write reviews or develop evaluation forms as aids for users assessing the programs and equipment.

Sale of Supplies

Some libraries sell computer-related supplies, such as blank disks, as a convenience to users. This is particularly appreciated when other supply sources are far away or not open as many hours as the library.

User Groups

The presence of microcomputer resources naturally results in the gathering of people interested in their use. The library can support this group interest by providing a location for regular meetings and perhaps even coordinate meeting schedules and agendas.

For example, a learning resources center librarian initiated an Authoring Systems Interest Group to bring together people involved in developing computer-assisted instruction in the health sciences. Some of the meetings were for informal communication and exchange of ideas; other meetings included presentations by educators, computer experts, and vendors.

SUMMARY

There are numerous services associated with public access microcomputer resources. Basic services are expected and should be provided wherever microcomputers are available for use. Other services are more specialized and enhance the library's role in supporting personal and institutional efforts to become proficient in the use of computer technology. The choice of specialized services often reflects the orientation of the library, the expertise of its staff, and the resources that are available.

Chapter Eight

Personnel

Managing public access microcomputer resources requires staff support. This chapter covers
- staff activities
- skills required to support these activities
- the role of the computer education specialist

No single factor, such as number of microcomputers present, defines the level of staff support required. The degree and type of support needed depend on many factors: the number of computers, the amount and kind of use, the size of the software collection, the place of microcomputers in the organization's activities and priorities, and the size and support needs of the user population. The presence of just a few computers does not necessarily imply little use, and the presence of many computers may result in more attention being directed to the equipment than to the users. The collection may have only a few unique programs in multiple copies; it may be primarily distributed through networks; or the collection may be large and varied and circulated as individual programs. Each of these characteristics has an effect on the kind of support needed by people using the resources.

The facilities and how they are used help determine the appropriate staffing configuration. For example, a computer lab open 24 hours a day with 50 computers requires different staffing than that of a 20-computer facility used primarily for class instruction. Organizational context is discussed in detail in Chapter Two (Funding); knowing where the service fits in the context of the broader organization is particularly important when planning and providing appropriate staff support.

This chapter discusses, in general, the types of skills and staff needed to support activities related to public access microcomputer resources and services. There is some overlap with topics discussed in other chapters, such as in Chapter Seven (User Services). The primary focus is on staff for the larger, academic public access microcomputer facility, but there are examples from different kinds of libraries. The lists of skills and activities that support public access microcomputer use are long but not mandatory. Each library must determine the appropriate mix of staff skills and activities necessary to support its specific microcomputer environment.

STAFF ACTIVITIES

The following lists major library staff activities associated with public access microcomputer resources:

- evaluating and selecting equipment and software
- purchasing and installing equipment and software
- upgrading/repairing equipment and software
- monitoring use
- cataloging software
- packaging software for use
- circulating software
- training staff
- consulting with users
- liaison to user groups
- promoting the use of facilities and services
- teaching
- managing networks
- planning
- providing justification for funding

This list includes traditional library functions, such as selection and cataloging, as well as nontraditional activities, such as network management and installation of equipment and software. Some activities, such as circulating software, require minimal training, whereas others are more complex and require specialized skills, such as teaching and network management. Depending on the type of library and services, one person may perform all of the computer-related activities or they may be distributed among people who specialize in one or more functions. In the small hospital library, the solo librarian may assume computer support activities along with other responsibilities. In many larger libraries, certain activities are distributed and integrated into existing staff positions, for example, the cataloging staff catalogs software.

GENERAL SKILLS

An obvious requirement for staff associated with any microcomputer activity is being "computer literate," defined here as being familiar with the basic operation and common uses of microcomputers and software. More students are now learning these skills as part of their general education, but it is still important to establish that an individual is familiar with, or will learn, the basics of microcomputers and their use before assuming responsibility for a microcomputer-related activity.

Catalogers often must use a program in order to describe it; circulation staff are sometimes the only staff available to provide assistance after normal working hours. Self-confidence, the quality of work, and user satisfaction can be adversely affected by a staff member's lack of understanding of the fundamentals of computing. This skill can be acquired on the job, in formal courses, or through self-instructional programs. The following is a sample checklist, from an Introduction to Computers Workbook, of objectives that indicate a minimal level of general computer literacy.

After finishing this introduction to computers, participants will be able to:

- identify the components of a computer system and their individual functions
- describe the keyboard and what individual keys are for
- boot and turn off the computer and its components correctly
- discuss the function of DOS and show how it is used
- identify types of computer software and recognize how they might be useful
- complete Exploring the IBM Personal Computer
- use two other software packages to become more familiar with the keyboard and printer.

(Indiana University School of Dentistry Library, used with permission)

Certain staff, who may or may not be librarians, need to know much more than just the basics. These are the people involved in providing direct educational support, such as teaching or consultation, as well as those providing equipment-related support, such as selection, installation, or maintenance. In addition to their technical expertise, they must appreciate the characteristics of the library environment in which computing takes place. An understanding and acceptance of the principles of shared access and service orientation and a commitment to supporting policies, such as those related to copyright, are important in all library staff, not just librarians.

DIRECT USER SUPPORT

Direct user support is clustered into three broad types of activities:
- frontline problem-solving assistance
- formal or informal instruction
- in-depth consultation

Frontline Problem-Solving Assistance

Frontline assistance consists of on-site, immediate help when a user has a problem or question. Some frontline assistance may be offered by the circulation staff, but this is usually limited to helping with basic operations such as starting up a program or identifying an equipment problem. It is unreasonable to expect circulation staff to provide considerable frontline problem-solving help unless everyone on the circulation staff has the expertise to provide a consistent level of service. If circulation staff provide help with computer use, they must decide when to interrupt circulation assistance to solve a problem and when to interrupt helping a user in order to provide circulation services. Since solving many user problems involves seeing the equipment, program, and particular problem firsthand, circulation staff may frequently be called away from their primary work area in order to provide assistance. Thus, dependence on circulation staff for frontline problem-solving coverage is not optimal.

In some schools, faculty arrange for graduate students to provide course-related computing support in the library. Or, computer center staff provide frontline assistance wherever there are computers, including in the library. The presence of nonlibrary staff on-site to provide direct user services requires clear definition of staff roles and supervision, good communication, and close cooperation between library and nonlibrary staff. Users should know what to expect from a staff member, should be appropriately referred if necessary, and should perceive that the service is integrated and adequate. For example, if a graduate teaching assistant is available only during certain scheduled hours and only to help students from a particular course complete their assignments, other users need to know not to expect extensive, if any, assistance from that person.

No user should be left without someone to turn to for help. More specialized services, such as programming support, may not be available, although whoever provides frontline support should also make appropriate referrals to people who provide these other services.

Some libraries house public access microcomputers that are administratively the responsibility of another department, such as the computer center. All staff in the facility should be supervised by library management since the resource is perceived as part of the library. Cooperative arrangements are discussed in more detail in Chapter Nine (Administrative Issues).

Instruction

The frontline problem-solver should be an expert, but may or may not be expected to teach. Teaching ranges from ad hoc individual instruction to formal classroom presentations. In public access microcomputer environments, there are numerous topics to cover including
- explaining what facilities and services are available
- describing possible microcomputer applications in a particular subject area
- demonstrating an example of computer-assisted instruction
- showing how to use a productivity software package, for example, how to set up a database

Reference service has always included instruction, formal and informal, but the introduction of microcomputers, and especially the development of end-user searching, has enhanced and increased the teaching role of library staff. Not everyone who knows a subject can, should, or wants to teach it. People new to teaching need guidance in how to do it and can get help from coursework, such as MLA's continuing education course "Teaching Strategies for the Medical Librarian," or by establishing a student-mentor relationship with an experienced instructor.

Both the content and format of teaching programs in libraries are evolving:

> The trend is in its early stages among corporate libraries, but already end-user education—including gateway training, searching specific databases, private database management, and *compact disc* technology—is underway. More emphasis on in-service education, cooperation with library schools, and peer education is also noticeable in the literature. As well as incorporating innovative subject matter and reaching new audiences, these newer educational programs are using formats hitherto unknown or little used for in-library teaching. The emphasis is on appropriate adult education technologies mounted to the economic advantage of each library. This calls for specialized planning and program management.[1]

Some librarians make use of computer technology to teach about computers. "Canned" presentations, in which computer interaction is simulated in a computer-generated slide show, computer-assisted tutorials, and *hypermedia* applications present alternatives to the lecture format. These programs can replace some of the effort of repetitive teaching, as well as individualize instruction. Of course, as in the case of most educational programs, the investment of time and money in development is usually substantial.

Consultation

Consultation involves giving in-depth expert advice. In microcomputer environments, individuals seek advice about many things: which program to use, what type of equipment to buy for home use, how best to enter data in a database, which database is most likely to meet certain information needs. Some questions can be addressed more efficiently with a handout or course. For example, information about routine activities, such as how to download files, can be presented in a fact sheet. Other questions are more complex and individualized, such as how to turn a personal research file into a departmental database.

Although many librarians have considerable expertise, particularly in structuring database input for retrieval, consultation projects such as creating a multiuser database from a personal file may require the expertise of more than one person. For example, a librarian may lack sufficient knowledge of the department's telecommunications system and need to consult with local telecommunications experts in order to help develop a departmental database. Effective consultation often involves identifying the areas outside one's own expertise and working in conjunction with other experts.

Consultation takes considerable time and commitment; it can become a full-time occupation. Informal consulting is not as controllable as teaching or reference assistance. It is important to define clearly what consultation does and does not involve, and to revise the consultant's list of job accountabilities to reflect this role and its relative priority.

Successful consulting can enhance status, which leads to more requests for consultation and raises issues about staff allocation. For example, one health sciences library has two full-time professionals and two part-time staff members to manage the library microcomputer facilities, assist users, and make house calls on campus to help users with microcomputer-related problems. On the other hand, consultation by an improperly informed person who gives bad advice can have a negative impact on the library's credibility.

STAFF FOR EQUIPMENT-RELATED SUPPORT

As users become more knowledgeable and as equipment becomes more powerful and plentiful, the level of dependence on computers and concern about system reliability increases. If the library is to be a central place for microcomputer resources, its equipment must work day in and day out. This implies some on-site equipment-related problem-solving support even if major repair and maintenance are provided by an outside service.

Equipment-related support skills are discussed separately from direct user support. However, equipment support is an integral part of direct user support, and the same staff often provide both. Chapters Four (Equipment and Peripherals) and Five (Local Area Networks) also cover aspects of equipment support activities.

Basic on-site equipment support includes
- identification of equipment problems
- routine maintenance
- liaison to external equipment vendors and service personnel
  On-site equipment support may also involve
- equipment installation
- equipment upgrade
- basic equipment repair
- local area network management

Identifying and Solving Equipment Problems

Computing is an activity combining people, equipment, and software. The typical first step in problem solving is to determine whether the problem is with the equipment, the software, or the person's use of the equipment or software. Library staff can learn to distinguish between an equipment or software problem and a problem with their use.

Routine Maintenance

Regular maintenance of computer equipment is discussed in Chapter Four (Equipment and Peripherals). Activities such as cleaning monitors and keyboards can be the ongoing responsibility of library volunteers, assistants, or student staff. In libraries that did not have audiovisual equipment prior to acquiring microcomputers, staff may have to learn the importance of regular equipment maintenance. Dirt and food around computers can cause operating problems, as well as make using the facility less pleasant.

Liaison to Vendors and Service Personnel

Many vendors and service personnel find public access use of microcomputer equipment in libraries out of the ordinary compared to most office and technical use. A specific person in the library needs to work closely with these people so that library needs can be met. That library staff person must have good technical and communication skills in order to explain how proposed or malfunctioning equipment must work in the library environment.

For example, a corporate medical library has the only public access CD-ROM unit in the organization. Getting the equipment installed involved educating computer personnel about how the system is used and how it is supposed to work. Although the technology is new to them, local computer center staff have the skills to figure out most of the equipment problems that arise. When there is a problem beyond their abilities, the librarian serves as either a referral point or interface to the CD-ROM vendor's technical services support person.

Liaison to external equipment and software vendors and service personnel requires solid understanding of what needs to be accomplished, good judgment about what is reasonable to expect, and persuasive persistence in getting the task done satisfactorily. Much of the job consists of gathering and comparing information about services and products. Working with equipment and software dealers can be an enjoyable challenge, but it is not for the retiring personality or the poor communicator. Equipment and software purchases and repair/maintenance agreements are usually contractual. The library representative must be aware of the scope of authority needed to make commitments on behalf of the organization and know who else must be consulted for approval. A logical, flexible, and creative approach in proposing "deals" and compromises helps, too.

Equipment Installation, Upgrade, and Repair

Computer equipment installation, upgrade, and repair are not activities approached with a wrench. One needs a thorough understanding of how that particular computer system works, of sophisticated diagnostics programs, and of the appropriate tools for the job at hand. Equipment purchase often includes a warranty period and the option of establishing a maintenance agreement. These contractual agreements should be reviewed before purchase and again before arranging for repair, upgrade, maintenance, or the installation of another component part. Unauthorized attempts at repair or modification may violate warranty agreements.

Libraries often have access to their institution's internal or contract computer repair services and depend on them for equipment repair rather than train or hire staff to meet these needs. If the library has staff members who are inclined and able to repair equipment, standards should be established regarding training and job responsibilities. Training opportunities for novices are varied. For example, one university computer center has an extensive self-paced training program for new computer center frontline consultants that includes the basics of equipment configuration and repair. When approached, the program director was quite willing to allow a library computer specialist to participate because he saw the advantage to his group of having more people on campus who understood enough to do basic diagnosis and repair.

Network Management

Networking computers can enhance the users' ability to access programs, transfer data, and communicate. Network features are discussed extensively in Chapter Five (Local Area Networks). But networks also establish significant systems interdependence; when the network, or one program on it, has a problem, all users may be hindered from doing work. If there are plans to install a network, provisions must be made for local network management to monitor the system and respond immediately to system problems.

One could argue that network management is a full-time job; it is certainly not a sideline responsibility when many users become dependent on the network. Network management encompasses varied and complex tasks requiring specialized knowledge such as establishing levels of access, installing software and creating front-end interfaces to it, locating breaks in communications, and monitoring network performance.

Network suppliers usually offer training for the local network manager. Because of the investment in training and experience, this is not a job to be passed on from one student, or temporary, employee to another. It is a job for a permanent staff member and may be in addition to other responsibilities with the understanding that the network takes priority. Backup staff is also strongly advised.

THE COMPUTER EDUCATION SPECIALIST

The considerable effort required to maintain a modern microcomputer resource center and to meet user demands prompts libraries and institutions with a high level of computing activity to add dedicated staff or expand the role of existing staff to support public access computing.

The nature of the demand for support varies among institutions and over time in the same institution. Ten microcomputers can lead to 20, then 40. The type of computer supported can change from IBM PC to IBM PS/2 to Macintosh or, more likely, all three at once. The same computer is upgraded again and again. Not too long ago, most users needed basic instruction; now many users know the fundamentals but need help using sophisticated programs and powerful, often integrated, systems. Software continues to improve, and users want access to the latest versions. Everyone expects the equipment to work all of the time. User demand brought microcomputers to many libraries, and the user's need for support creates a demand for personnel.

The staff skills necessary to support public access computing are varied and difficult to find in a single person. The person who deals effectively with vendors may not be the same person who best teaches users how to construct a database. As a result, many computer-related staff activities are initially distributed among existing staff. Piecing together the time of many staff members may get the immediate job done, but it does not allow for the broad vision, accountability, and commitment that come with being primarily responsible for a service. Staff who are dedicated to a particular service can focus on how the service is used and how it can be improved.

There has been a trend to create positions in libraries for staff who are primarily responsible for public access computer activities. That position is sometimes called "computer education specialist," indicating emphases on both the technology and the process of using, or learning to use, it.

Job Description

The library computer education specialist role is a balance among technician, educator, and information expert. There are many career paths, educational and practical, that can develop the skills needed to do the job. The job itself probably consists of activities similar to those listed at the beginning of this chapter. A particular job's primary focus depends on the local environment and the institution's needs. The job may have components of reference, systems, or media librarian duties. Since computer-related environments change, both the position and the person filling it should be flexible. This section offers suggestions, using examples, for writing job descriptions that attract people with the needed skills and that define the job without restricting its development. Excerpts from actual job descriptions are included.

There are useful resources for writing job descriptions, some of which are listed at the end of this chapter. Most institutions have their own guidelines as well. Unlike some established library jobs where the content of the work is similar across different institutions (reference services, for example), the work of a staff person who supports public access microcomputer use is not universally understood nor is it the same work in all environments. Job announcements use a variety of job titles including "Computer Education Specialist," "Microcomputer Consultant," "Computer Services Librarian," and "Systems Librarian."

Staff positions to help people use microcomputer resources are relatively new and still being defined. Therefore, it is important that the job description clearly define the major responsibilities and performance expectations, leaving little room for misunderstanding about what the job involves. Examples of responsibilities include

- manage Novell local area network
- provide assistance to computer users, including answering hardware and software questions
- teach courses on computer applications
- prepare software for circulation/distribution

What follows is a sample list of responsibilities arranged by category:

Management
- enforces microcomputer use rules
- prepares statistical reports
- orders supplies
- maintains computer use schedules
- writes user policies
- prepares annual hardware and software budget
- develops security procedures
- promotes the service (PR)
- maintains inventory control
- plans for future needs and new services

Hardware Expertise
- troubleshoots hardware problems
- performs routine hardware maintenance
- manages a LAN
- manages a bulletin board service
- manages a library-site network
- coordinates a library network with outside systems

Software Expertise
- troubleshoots software
- copies software onto a hard disk
- writes user-menus
- writes user access instructions
- makes backup copies of software
- manages a LAN
- manages a bulletin board service
- manages a library-wide network
- coordinates a library network with outside systems

Education
- assists users with software (DOS or applications)

- assists users with hardware
- provides end-user search assistance
- develops computer skills courses
- teaches computer skills courses
- works with faculty to integrate micros into curriculum
- consults regarding hardware and software needs
- trains library staff
- consults in database design
- provides one-on-one user assistance

Library Skills
- recommends software titles for purchase
- evaluates and selects software titles
- selects books for computer reference
- catalogs computer software

(Damon Camille, MLA New Perspectives Series "Managing Microcomputers," used with permission)

Qualifications vary, but frequently cited ones are
- familiarity with microcomputer hardware and software (systems and programs specified)
- experience in a teaching or information services environment
- effective oral and written communication skills

Because the job includes working both with equipment and with people, technical competence and a service orientation are required. The following are samples of job responsibilities and qualifications listed in actual job descriptions:

Microcomputer Consultant

Responsibilities:
1. Oversee the daily operation of the NML Microcomputer Facility, including maintaining supplies, arranging for equipment repairs, installing equipment, etc.
2. Assist USC faculty, students, and staff in using microcomputer hardware and software belonging to the Library, including giving brief training sessions.
3. Prepare new software for addition to the NML collection, including making backup copies, installing software for NML equipment, and creating self-booting programs.
4. Perform other projects and responsibilities as assigned.

Qualifications:
Requires basic knowledge of microcomputer usage, including proper disk handling, booting up a microcomputer, basic IBM DOS commands, and having used a microcomputer for at least one application previously. Also requires good oral and written communication skills and the ability to work with the public.

(University of Southern California Norris Medical Library, used with permission)

Microcomputer Lab Specialist

Responsibilities:

1. With the Collection Development Librarian, has responsibility for selecting and maintaining Microlab software and computer books within the limits of the Microlab budget. Maintains accounting records for that budget.
2. Plans, designs, and teaches informal and formal instructional programs and materials for Microlab users in DOS, WordPerfect, dBASE, Lotus, etc.
3. Maintains and updates all Microlab publications, promotional materials, and instructional manuals including: Microlab policy and procedure manual, software column for the Library newsletter, *Information at a Glance*, cheat sheets, and bulletin boards.
4. With AVSC Manager, gives Microlab orientations and demonstrations and recommends policies and procedures for daily operations of the Lab.
5. Maintains statistics and submits quarterly, semi-annual, and annual reports.
6. Troubleshoots microcomputer hardware and software problems for IIS staff.
7. Provides formal and informal instructional programs for IIS staff on software applications.
8. Maintains microcomputer and printer supplies for IIS department.
9. Makes recommendations for new microcomputer equipment purchase in writing to Assistant Director, IIS, including obtaining three bids.
10. Is responsible for the installation and evaluation of new CAI, videodisc, CD-ROM, and other microcomputer instructional programs including but not limited to: InfoWindow, the Match, Physiology Lab, Pathology and Anatomy Videodisc, MEDLINE and Science Citation Index Compact Disc Edition.
11. Is responsible for installing, testing of, and training on new equipment purchased for use by IIS staff.
12. Other duties and special projects as assigned such as, but not limited to, providing Reference Desk coverage and participating in providing online searches using a variety of database systems and vendors.

Qualifications:

Master's Degree in Library or Information Science and at least 3 to 5 years experience in a biomedical library with Reference Desk and online searching or equivalent degree in Computer and Information Science or Education/Educational Technology with at least 3 years work or teaching experience with microcomputers in an academic environment required. Familiarity with a variety of microcomputer hardware (Apple IIe, Macintosh, IBM-PC) and software (WordPerfect, WordStar, dBASE, Lotus) desired. Excellent skills in program development, program evaluation, teaching, writing and oral communication are essential.

(George Washington University Paul Himmelfarb Health Sciences Library, used with permission)

Learning Center Librarian

Responsibilities:
Under the direction of the Head of Public Services, the Learning Center Librarian's responsibilities include managing the operations and collections of the Learning Center; supervising one full-time Library Assistant and student assistants; selecting media and software; assisting in developing departmental policies; developing and implementing departmental procedures; promoting effective utilization of facilities, equipment, and resources, including provision of information and instructional services; assisting library staff in selecting and learning to use software appropriate to their specific applications.

Qualifications:
MLS from an ALA-accredited Graduate Library School required. Four years experience in a health sciences or academic library, including significant experience with microcomputers, both Macintosh and IBM; technical competence and an indepth knowledge of DOS and a variety of applications software. Reference and online experience and experience in teaching adult learners desired.

(University of Rochester Medical Center Edward G. Miner Library, used with permission)

Systems Coordinator

Responsibilities:
Responsibilities will include the following: Managing Local Area Network(s) within the LRC, including an IBM Token Ring Network; training and supervising student computer consultants (2.00 FTE); recommending microcomputer hardware and software; facilitating use of computer resources within the LRC; assisting in planning and presentation of workshops related to computer hardware, software, and applications; and assisting library staff in computer-related activities.

Qualifications:
1. ALA-accredited MLS or other appropriate Master's degree, such as Information Systems/Science or Health Informatics.

2. Excellent interpersonal and communication skills.
3. Significant experience with microcomputers including Macintosh and IBM personal computers and commercially available software.

(University of Minnesota Bio-Medical Library, used with permission)

Assistant Medical Librarian

Responsibilities:
The assistant librarian will develop an audiovisual collection, manage the CAI collection, and oversee the installation of a library computer system.

Qualifications:
Experience in a health sciences library, ability to search online databases, and familiarity with library computer applications. MLS is essential with MLA certification desirable.

(Winthrop-University Hospital, used with permission)

Funding

Funding is discussed more generally and extensively in Chapter Two (Funding). The discussion here is limited to funding for a computer education specialist position. As with any staff position, funding for this position requires justification. The obvious justification is user demand, which usually is easier to document for computer support than, for instance, cataloging support because the activity more immediately involves users. But because so many things related to computers change, the institution may be reluctant to commit to a permanent position even when there is currently a high demand for service.

Funding may be partial and/or temporary with the mandate to prove lasting value over time before the position is made permanent. Territoriality among departments within an institution can affect funding for personnel. Given that the job needs to be done, who will get the money and position: the library, the computer center, or the department or school that wants user support? Cooperative funding arrangements can be made with the agreement that supervision is most appropriately based in the library where the work is done and can be evaluated. In return, library administration must be willing to assume the responsibility and effort of supervision. Cooperative arrangements are also discussed in Chapters Two (Funding) and Nine (Administrative Issues).

Recruitment and Selection

There are many ways to acquire the skills needed to support public access microcomputer resources use and many groups from which to attract candidates, such as

- librarians
- educators
- computer scientists
- health sciences professionals

The type of candidates sought depends on the focus of the position. Librarians may be more appropriate for a position that involves overall management, software selection, and service development. A computer scientist or otherwise technically oriented individual may be a better choice for a position that is primarily consulting and computer maintenance and repair. Students or other part-time workers may be good choices for front-line consulting that primarily involves a basic knowledge of computers.

Coursework or experience with microcomputers is, of course, essential. The employer will have to determine if the coursework and/or experience is suitable for the job from the resume and the interview. A few salient questions can help determine a candidate's level of technical sophistication and awareness of future trends. Sample questions are:

- What computer-related magazines do you scan regularly?
- What steps would you follow to resolve a problem a user is having printing a WordPerfect file?
- What computer system, described in detail, do you have at home or would you recommend for home purchase?
- Do you know of any way to protect files on a hard disk?

Many people now use microcomputers and may consider themselves expert because they know one system very well. Being a so-called hacker on a single system does not qualify one for a job that involves working with people who are using computers. Including a "typical" user in the interview process or asking a few questions typical of users, for example, "I want to use a word processing program; what do you suggest?" may provide insight into how the candidate might interact with users on the job.

If the person is expected to teach, provide an opportunity during the interview for the candidate to teach something simple, such as how to handle a floppy disk.

Many on-site computer experts end up helping with other library computer projects. Make sure the candidate has an opportunity to learn about the total library environment and understands how the job fits in that environment.

The position may be multifaceted, and most candidates will have areas of strength and areas of weakness. A rating sheet that lists the primary job skills can help sort out the candidate with the overall best score for the need at hand. Figures 8.1 and 8.2 are examples of rating sheets and checklists that can be adapted for use.

Figure 8.1 Skills Rating Worksheet

Microcomputer Education Specialist Skills Rating

Skill	Rating Poor ↔ Excellent			
Technical expertise				
Microcomputer	1	2	3	4
Software	1	2	3	4
Operating systems	1	2	3	4
Local area network	1	2	3	4
Communication skills				
Written	1	2	3	4
Oral	1	2	3	4
Teaching skills	1	2	3	4

Figure 8.2 Detailed Interview Worksheet

Consultant Interview

Name of applicant _____

School and major _____ Year in school _____

Rating Scale:

1 Strongly agree/Outstanding
2 Agree/Clearly acceptable
3 Disagree/Probably unacceptable

4 Strongly disagree/ Clearly unacceptable
5 Neutral/Not applicable

Rating/Comments

Computer Experience

Experience with several types of computers _____
Familiar and comfortable with PC DOS _____
Experience in using user-oriented computers _____
Familiar with Mainframe operating system _____
Capable of simple programming in at least
  one of BASIC, *Pascal,* or *FORTRAN* _____
Hardware expertise _____
Specialized computer skills _____

Software Expertise

Experience with a variety of software applications _____
Experience with a wordprocessor or text editor _____
Familiar with the basic concept of spreadsheets _____
Operationally familiar with spreadsheets _____
Familiar with electronic mail _____
Experience with file transfer/communications software _____
Specialized software skills _____

Figure 8.2 Detailed Interview Worksheet (*continued*)

Service Experience

Experience in a service-oriented capacity _____

Experience in a teaching capacity _____

Experience in individual instruction or tutoring _____

Experience working on committees or group projects _____

Specialized service-oriented skills or experience _____

Personal Attributes

Experience in unsupervised environments _____

Eager to learn new software and hardware _____

Long-term goals involve people and/or computers _____

Explains things about him/herself in an organized and clear manner _____

Evidences appropriate social skills during interview _____

Evidences professionalism during interview _____

The applicant appears well-groomed and dressed appropriately for
   a Stanford interview _____

General impression of ability to interact with users _____

Overall Assessment (Not a summation of above, an overall impression) _____

Recommended Action   _____   _____   _____
                        Hire   Hold for future   Do not hire
                                     consideration

Obtain further information (specify which kind)

_____

_____

Interviewers' Signatures _____

_____

Comments _____

_____

_____

(Stanford University Graduate School of Business Computing Facility, used with permission)

Salary Issues

Hiring a computer education specialist raises other personnel issues, especially when the specialist is not a professional librarian. Where does the computer education specialist fit within the library's personnel structure? Is this a professional position? What if the individual hired does not have a master's level degree? Salary for the technically skilled individual may need to be at a professional level to attract competent people from the computer industry. Technically skilled librarians are not as prevalent as librarians with other skills. Higher salaries may be required to attract the appropriate candidates.

INVOLVEMENT OF OTHER LIBRARY STAFF

Computer use is no longer the special domain of computer experts. Librarians use microcomputers for word processing, database access, data analyses, and for information management. Librarians may, relative to other job responsibilities, contribute many specialized skills to support public access microcomputer resources use. Technical services staff can bring cataloging expertise to organizing the software collection and can also contribute their information-management skills to library-sponsored courses on building bibliographic databases. Database searchers may be in great demand to assist people who want to use microcomputers to access outside information services. If the library's CD-ROM or database search station is located with the rest of the microcomputers in a separate area, reference librarians will probably be called upon to support their use. Library administrators play an important role in the continued development of the resource, as well as in their interaction with representatives of user groups and other administrators who are involved with providing computer-related services. Everyone in the library can have a role in supporting the use of public access microcomputer resources.

SUMMARY

Staff support for the provision and use of public access microcomputer resources is critical. Activities and skills vary from teaching users to installing equipment, managing networks, establishing policies, and planning new services. Libraries that become involved in providing access to microcomputers may have to assess current staff skills, provide more staff training opportunities, reassign job responsibilities, advocate for additional staff, and incorporate personnel from other disciplines.

Reference
1. Zachert MJK. Educational services in special libraries: planning and administration. Chicago:Medical Library Association, 1990, 6.

Additional Resources
Position descriptions in health sciences libraries. MLA DocKit #1. Chicago:Medical Library Association, 1989.
Writing library job descriptions. ALA TipKit #7. Chicago:American Library Association/OLPR, 1985.
Association of Research Libraries
  1527 New Hampshire Avenue, NW
  Washington, DC 20036
  SPEC Center (202) 232-8656 (Publications and Job Descriptions)

Chapter Nine
Administrative Issues

This chapter takes a broad view of various issues related to providing public access microcomputer resources. Our intent is to identify issues not already covered in conjunction with more specific topics, such as equipment and software, and to elaborate on the administrative aspects of topics previously covered. Reference to related chapters is provided when appropriate; the index is also a source for identifying issues not mentioned in this chapter.

Administrative issues discussed in this chapter include

- access
- fees
- security
- statistics
- institutional involvement
- staff development
- cooperative arrangements
- changing technology

ACCESS

Extended hours of availability are important to many computer users. Security concerns and user support needs mandate that access to computer equipment be supervised in all but the most controlled environments. (Staff members in a hospital, for example, might have keyed access to library resources, including computers.) In large institutions, the library users may demand extended hours of operation just to use the computers.

Some libraries physically isolate the computer facility, making access to the equipment possible when other areas of the library are closed. Remote access to library systems through a network is an alternative to providing on-site access to library computer equipment and software after normal hours of operation. Local area networks and after-hours access are discussed in Chapter Five (Local Area Networks). Some libraries are in organizations that have other, nonlibrary computer labs that maintain extended hours of service. In that case, coordination with and referral to the other labs are important user services.

Deciding who may use computers and software, and for how long, requires thoughtful review of policies and of the reasons why computer resources are present in a particular library. Clearly defined circulation policies and procedures, based on the overall mission of the library, minimize unanticipated and undesired use of the resources. For example, priority use might be given to people using software in conjunction with class assignments if a primary goal of the library is to support the curriculum. As another example, priority use might be given to the library's primary user population, such as medical students or housestaff, although others would have access to the equipment when it was not being used by someone from the priority group.

Librarians should be wary about accepting responsibility for public access microcomputers under the condition that they are available to only selected groups of library users. Discriminatory circulation policies detract from the library's role as an institutional service promoting shared access to limited resources.

Use may be limited to a specified period of time with renewal allowed only if no one is waiting to use the equipment. Computers can be equipped with keyed power sources or keyboards so that a key must be checked out to the user. Checking out keys controls access and makes it easier to establish a time period of use. For instance, perhaps only people with valid institutional identification can check out a key, which is due back in two hours. This policy defines who can use the equipment and for how long. In some networked environments, checking out a computer can be done by signing onto the network with valid identification; the network administrator can monitor time on the system, terminating access when the specified time is up. Controlled access, monitored either by people or systems, equitably distributes use and has the added benefit of making it easier to gather use statistics. Access and use policies should be clearly defined and posted.

Example
Microcomputer Skills Lab Policies
1. Use of computers restricted to HAM-TMC Library card holders, and card-eligible employees of supporting institutions
2. No games allowed
3. No food or drink allowed in the MSL
4. All users must sign in before using computers
5. Patrons who do not sign in may be asked to give up computers
6. Reservations are for two hours only
7. Computers and software can be reserved one week in advance
8. Computers and software can be reserved a maximum of two times a day, with at least two hours between reservations
9. Reservations will be held for 15 minutes only
10. No software should be copied, except for titles designated as "shareware" or "public domain"; violators will be prohibited from using MSL hardware and software

11. We only offer limited assistance with programming
12. Limited assistance (with booting, paper, ribbons, jammed print-ers) is available after 6:00 PM and on weekends
13. Patrons must supply their own storage disks
14. All software must be used in the LRC
15. We cannot offer assistance with software not owned by the LRC
16. Only one computer can be checked out at a time
17. Only one software title can be checked out at a time (exceptions for programs used in tandem, e.g., PFS:Write & PFS:Proof)
18. Users must save their work and sign off 15 minutes before the Library closes

(Houston Academy of Medicine-Texas Medical Center Library, used with permission)

Example
Usage of CAI Programs

- One program (or part of a program) may be used at a time
- You will be asked to leave an identification (a license or school/work ID) before being given a program. Reading and signing a request form is also required. The materials will be listed on the request form, and returned materials checked against the list before the identification is returned
- No more than two people will be allowed to work together at a computer
- The computers are for CAI usage only

(National Library of Medicine Learning Resource Center, used with permission)

Other examples of access and use policy statements are given in Chapter Seven (User Services).

Access by disabled persons, including those with visual, fine motor, or orthopedic disabilities, should be considered. Legal requirements specified in the Federal Rehabilitation Act of 1973 state:

No otherwise qualified handicapped individual in the United States, . . . shall, solely by reason of his or her handicap, be excluded from the participation in, be denied the benefit of, or be subjected to discrimi-nation under any program receiving Federal financial assistance.[1]

Section 508 amendments to the act, codified as 29 U.S.C. Sec. 794d, spe-cifically provide for access by disabled persons to computer facilities. Al-though this requirement pertains only to federal agencies, it may extend to those receiving federal funding and, at the very least, it signals federal recognition of the issue.[2] Adaptations for the disabled may include mod-ifying facilities, for example, installing wheelchair ramps or changing key-board height and position. Other adaptations may involve changing soft-ware or hardware to provide larger characters to be displayed and printed;

to alter keyboard function to eliminate key repeat or allow for simultaneous typing of the shift, control, or escape keys with other keys; or to provide intelligent word processors that predict words or correct spelling or grammatical errors.

FEES

Computer equipment and software are expensive; users typically expect the latest features and versions. The introduction of microcomputers into libraries forces most librarians to reexamine fee-for-service issues.

Microcomputer resources are not unique to libraries; other institutional units may also provide access to microcomputers. It is important to assess all options available to users and to take these into account when determining whether or not, or how much, to charge. For example, some institutions impose computer fees for access to computer labs. If this fee does not pertain to library computer equipment, should the library also charge an access fee to be consistent with other available services? Can the library afford to have the only "free" access computers around without being forced to limit use in other ways—by user population, for example?

Fees can be imposed on the entire user population, as a one-time charge, or they can be collected in a pay-as-you-go method by direct charges for services such as the number of pages printed or the length of time the equipment is used. One-time charges usually require less administrative effort; pay-as-you-go methods can control wasteful or excessive usage.

Many people assume that charging is a way to make money. It is true that charging can do more than recover costs. But one should not forget the hidden expense of charging, including the costs of administration, verification, and record keeping. Also, one needs to determine whether the fees collected would directly benefit the library's computer budget, or if they are contributions to other, perhaps nonlibrary, budgets. Generally, institutional computing fees are not managed by libraries, and direct service fees, such as for printing, are used as a way to recover direct costs.

SECURITY AND SAFETY

Computer equipment must be secured from theft, damage, and unauthorized reconfiguration so that it performs reliably. Security devices for equipment are discussed in Chapter Four (Equipment and Peripherals); software security is discussed in Chapters Five (Local Area Networks) and Six (Software Collections). Antitheft strategies should not discourage legitimate use or impede repair. Of course, computer equipment should be inventoried regularly and included on insurance policies.

Preventing system and software tampering and modification can be difficult. The most effective control is to know who is doing what when; this is not usually feasible. Checking software when it is returned requires more time, and expertise, than the typical service desk staff has. One option is to adopt a policy that makes the person returning the software responsible for documented problems experienced by the next user. But proving that someone caused a problem and holding that person accountable after the material has been returned and loaned again is difficult, if not impossible. Service desk staff should at least check to see that all of the physical pieces are present before a program is returned to the shelf.

It is important to have policies and procedures in place to address cases of willful destruction of library materials, including microcomputer resources. The policy may be to impose a fine, charge replacement costs, deny borrowing and access privileges, or refer cases of tampering to the institution's disciplinary authorities.

Security concerns extend to the user's right, within reasonable institutional policies, to be assured that work done in the library is confidential. If a network saves files or monitors use, it should do so in ways that maintain the privacy of the user. If users are able to store files on a hard disk, they should be informed about the lack of security and protection of those files.

Library staff and users have the right to assume that their work environment is safe. The concentration of expensive equipment, late-night hours of access, the presence of cash registers if supplies are sold, and high volume use make public access microcomputer labs environments that may require more attention to security. Library administration should review staffing patterns to ensure that late-night staffing is adequate to meet service demand and provide an appropriate presence of authority. Additional staff or more regular patrol by security personnel may be needed. The high concentration of equipment also means that electrical cords can be underfoot and peripherals can be stacked on carts or in other precarious configurations. Chapter Three (Planning Facilities) discusses strategies for safely securing equipment; it is important to keep the facility free of hazards.

STATISTICS

Every significant library service should be monitored to provide information about how and how much the service is used. The level of detail in record keeping should reflect the importance of the indicator being measured. A couple of books about methods for documenting library use are listed at the end of this chapter. There are also computer network utilities that assist in gathering statistics about computer and software use.

Parent institutions, consortia, and professional organizations may regularly request information about microcomputer resources and their use. The Association of Academic Health Sciences Library Directors (AAHSLD) includes questions about public access microcomputers, networked terminals, and software in its yearly survey.[3] And, for planning purposes, it is always beneficial to have a good understanding of how existing resources are used and how use changes over time. See figure 9.1 for the types of questions typical of surveys and useful to the planning process.

Figure 9.1 Survey Questions

How many microcomputers? _____
Type of microcomputers? _____
How many people use the computers? _____
What percentage of use is by:
  people using their own software _____
  people using library software _____
What percentage of use is for:
  word processing _____
  computer-assisted instruction _____
  CD-ROM access _____
  spreadsheet _____
  connection to a network or mainframe _____
What is the yearly budget for:
  equipment _____
  software _____
  maintenance _____
  salaries _____
How many staff positions are dedicated to supporting
microcomputer resources? _____
Which of the following support services are offered and at
  what percentage of a full-time position are they
  provided:
  basic assistance, direction (less than 10 minutes) _____
  in-depth assistance (10 or more minutes) _____
  programming support _____
  formal instruction, classes _____
  on-site repair, upgrade _____
  network management _____
  circulation services _____
  cataloging _____
  software evaluation _____
Who uses the microcomputer resources?
  (percentage breakdown for local demographic categories:
  staff, students, faculty) _____

How many hours per week are microcomputer resources:
  available for use _____
  available for use with someone on-site to help _____
What are the funding sources to support which microcomputer resources and
  activities:
  library budget pays $_____ for _____
  institutional budget pays $_____ for _____
  user fees pay $_____ for _____
  direct service fees pay $_____ for _____
  grants pay $_____ for _____

A graphic representation of statistics can be useful in identifying a trend or supporting a proposal. For example, figures 9.2 and 9.3 document both the tremendous increase in computer-assisted instruction from one year to the next and the relative displacement of audiovisuals by the use of software over a period of five years.

INSTITUTIONAL INVOLVEMENT

The widespread dissemination of information and computer technology raises questions about the library's identity and role as a primary source of information. Not only should the health sciences library continue to be a main source of information, the library should also have a central role in an institution's efforts to manage its information resources. Reasons for the library to become involved in providing public access microcomputer resources are discussed in Chapter One (Incorporating Microcomputers into the Library). This section focuses on the library's role in computer-related activities within a larger organizational context.

Committee Participation

Whenever feasible, librarians should take advantage of opportunities to participate on committees responsible for the institution's information activities. Issues such as institutional computer budgets, resource availability, and computer applications can be common ground for administrators,

Figure 9.2 Example of a Graph Showing Computer-Assisted Instruction Utilization

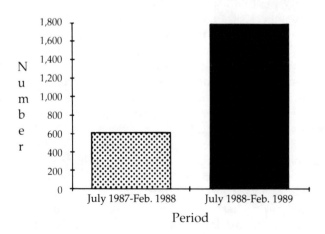

(University of Michigan, Learning Resource Center, used with permission)

Figure 9.3. Example of a Graph Showing Media Utilization

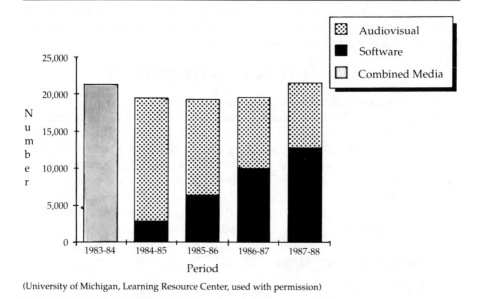

(University of Michigan, Learning Resource Center, used with permission)

providers, and users. Librarians may fit into any, or all three, of these roles, as well as the special role of user advocate if the library includes public access microcomputers. Institutional committee participation is also an opportunity to enhance library visibility and improve public relations, since most members of an organization are also part of the library user population. By meeting with nonlibrarian colleagues, one can learn more about general information needs and awareness of library services.

With the increased interest in computer-assisted instruction (CAI), representation on curriculum committees can be important, even essential, if the library is the main location where students use CAI programs. A librarian can report to the committee issues that arise related to the use of CAI materials, and work with faculty to evaluate the teaching value of the programs and to plan the development of new resources.

For example, the learning resources center librarian of an academic health sciences library served as an ad hoc member of the medical school's Internal Medicine Clerkship Committee. As a participant, she could assist the committee in purchase decisions for online search workstations to be placed in each of the affiliated teaching hospitals. By recommending the components of a workstation and assuming responsibility for coordinating the distribution of equipment, the library was identified as a resource for technology.

Maintaining a Central Role

The impact of computers on information access and management has been so significant that libraries may benefit from reassessing the priority of existing services in relationship to services associated with computer technology. Public access microcomputer resources represent more than just an addition to library service; for some users their availability is the main reason to use the library.

By making microcomputer resources and computer expertise priority library services, the library's orientation and identity may shift from that of a collection-based operation to one highlighting learning and information management. Library staff can support this reorientation at many levels, from developing handouts with information about equipment and software operation, to placing priority on helping users who have questions about using the microcomputer resources, to teaching classes about the use of the computers or specific software programs.

For example, the head of a dental school library decided that supporting microcomputer use was a priority library service. She is available to help users as needed and finds that approximately 20 percent of her time is spent teaching students and faculty how to use equipment and software. It is her impression that this effort enhances the library's image as an exciting and important educational resource.

By making support of public access microcomputers a priority service, the library can become the primary point of this service in an institution. Before working toward this identity, though, it is important to assess its long-term implications, including the need for a commitment to upgrade or replace equipment, purchase new versions of software, and develop and maintain a level of staff expertise to keep up with the technology. Many libraries got involved with providing public access microcomputers when training and computer literacy were the main concerns of users. Users, equipment, and software have become more sophisticated. Libraries that intend to play a central role in computer activities beyond that of supporting computer literacy will be expected to have current technology and software and, most importantly, staff who know more than just the basics.

STAFF DEVELOPMENT

It is essential that librarians keep up with changes in computer technology and applications. Regarding computer equipment and software as merely collections to be provided and maintained ignores the fact that computers represent a significant advance in information management and are new tools of the librarian's trade. As information professionals, librarians should have professional interest and involvement in using computers and working with others to learn more about them. Libraries need to support this effort.

Many librarians have taken advantage of opportunities to become more knowledgeable about and involved in computer-related activities. One reads about librarian computer consultants, librarians teaching courses about database management software, and librarians writing software reviews. Since microcomputers are relatively new, many librarians learned about them on the job. On-the-job training continues to be an important source of knowledge in this area.

Additional sources of information include postgraduate degree programs, such as the Training in Medical Informatics programs funded by the National Library of Medicine and offered at seven universities; individual postdoctoral fellowships funded by NLM; formal courses in computer science, information science, and education; seminars and workshops about specific equipment and software programs; user groups; and computer bulletin board services.

Conferences, such as EDUCOM and the Symposium on Computer Applications in Medical Care (SCAMC), bring together people interested in the application of computer technology. The publications and meetings of professional associations such as the Medical Library Association (MLA) and the American Society for Information Science (ASIS) contain information about computers in the health sciences. MLA's Educational Media and Technologies Section and the Medical Informatics Section encourage members to share information about computers in health sciences libraries. Computer trade shows and vendor product announcements offer opportunities to see many new products and to talk with vendors.

Being even generally informed about computer technology means keeping up with a great deal of information. Regular review of mainstream computer journals, such as *Byte* and *PC Magazine,* and newspapers, such as *InfoWorld,* at least keeps one aware of major trends. There are several specialty journals, *CD-ROM Librarian, MD Computing,* and *The Laserdisk Professional,* for example, that focus on specific aspects of computer technology and applications.

COOPERATIVE ARRANGEMENTS

Microcomputers are tools that make it possible for people of diverse backgrounds to store, manipulate, analyze, manage, and retrieve data and information. Microcomputers, peripherals, and software are also very expensive resources. As a result, there are often opportunities for librarians to work with nonlibrarians on projects that use microcomputers, and there are often situations in which cooperative funding or management arrangements make microcomputer resources available in organizations.

Cooperative projects between individuals can take many forms depending on one's level of skill and interest. Librarians with the appropriate knowledge can consult in the design of local databases, team teach courses in the use of software packages, or collaborate with faculty to develop instructional software. Librarians, through their education and experience, are particularly knowledgeable about information management and retrieval systems. When that expertise is recognized and appreciated outside of the library, library staff will probably be included in groups responsible for developing databases within the parent organization. One might consider it a professional, as well as fiscal, responsibility to offer this expertise as a resource to the larger organization.

For example, when data processing personnel in a pharmaceutical corporation recognized that the company's librarians had significant experience with large text databases and retrieval systems, the librarians were invited to participate in discussions about a company-wide information directory. In those discussions, the directory was described as "like a library catalog." Librarians provided the basis of the proposed format for the information to be included. In the next phase of the project, a librarian was asked to chair an interdivisional and multidisciplinary team to develop a prototype. One of the project's sponsors for implementation is the company's library planning group.

Organizational cooperative arrangements can be very successful, as in the case of the library that gets equipment and equipment support from the computer center, but assumes administrative responsibility and has funding for staff and services. Each cooperative agreement is unique and must be negotiated carefully in good faith and with contingency plans. A certain amount of ambiguity and shared ownership may be necessary to encourage "buy in," but one must not give away, in the name of cooperation, the library's ability to meet its own unique obligations to users and to the parent organization. The primary success factors cited in the discussion of a collaborative arrangement between a library and a microcomputer support center were

- complementary missions
- mutually beneficial outcomes
- emphasis on process vs. structure
- formal service agreement
- compatible management philosophies

The limiting factors cited were

- divergent missions
- territoriality
- overlapping lines of authority[4]

The placement of microcomputers in the library is often the result of a cooperative arrangement. In most organizations, space is at a premium. The library, because of its central location and identity as a common work space, may be seen as the most likely place to install public access microcomputers. Sharing space with the computer center in return for availability of microcomputers on-site can be a successful strategy to meet the objective of providing access to microcomputer resources. But, the library should retain the option to reclaim the space if future library needs and objectives change, or if the arrangement is not successful from the library's viewpoint. And, as mentioned above, the lines of authority, as well as responsibility, need to be defined in a formal agreement with contingency plans.

For example, computer center microcomputers were placed in the learning resources center of a library. The computer center staffed the lab but, within a year, funding for staff ceased although the microcomputers remained. Users assumed that learning center staff, by proximity, would be knowledgeable and provide support. The library administration's choice was either to close the lab or to reallocate other library resources in order to support it. In the interim, the library was identified with marginal service even though it was not officially responsible for the lab.

In another case, the university computer center proposed placing 50 microcomputers, a software collection, and staff in a health sciences library, converting the space into a microcomputer lab similar to others established around the campus. The lab would be a campus resource, available to all registered students. The library's administration declined the proposal on the basis that the health sciences library is a specialized environment and that space within it should be allocated to encourage the use of all library resources by its primary clientele.

Providing access to microcomputer resources may become a priority for a library, but a library is too valuable an environment to turn into just a place to go to use computers. Instead, all of the library's resources—the collections, the expertise of staff, the policies that encourage sharing resources—can and should enhance the use of microcomputers. Cooperative arrangements related to microcomputers ought to support the library's overall mission.

CHANGING TECHNOLOGY

Computer resources are expensive. Added to this, computer technology continues to evolve at such a rapid pace that the technology purchased today predictably will not be considered adequate in five years. Most organizations are not in the habit of making large capital investments for items of short-lived effectiveness. Many administrators have paid dearly for misadventures in "chasing" the latest technology that resulted in an assortment of incompatible pieces of equipment too costly to abandon and too cumbersome to use. As mentioned in Chapter Four (Equipment and Peripherals), the decision to replace equipment should be prompted by significant improvements; otherwise, it might be better to try to upgrade existing equipment.

Even if a library could always afford the most current equipment and software, it would not benefit library users to have to deal with so many changes all of the time. To some extent, a library needs to provide a predictable environment so that library users can know what to expect and how to use the resources. But there is a place for innovation, even when most of the resources remain the same. The library can serve as a beta test site for new software, or designate one workstation for more advanced or specialized use, such as for interactive videodisc or as a CD-ROM workstation.

During this chaotic time of rapid advances in technology, the library must balance the need to standardize resources for the majority of uses while continuing to offer resources that reflect improvements.

SUMMARY

Public access microcomputer resources in the library require administrative oversight and support. Because computer technology is new, expensive, and of widespread interest, it is particularly important that librarians make thoughtful decisions about integrating computers with other library services and evaluate the impact of computers on other library resources.

References
1. 29 U.S.C. Sec. 794.
2. Brill J. Access and opportunity: section 508. EDUCOM Review 1989 Summer;24(2):27–31.
3. Annual statistics of medical school libraries in the United States and Canada. Houston: Association of Academic Health Sciences Library Directors, 1978–.
4. Jenkins CG. Success factors for providing collaborative microcomputer information support services. Annual Meeting of the Medical Library Association, Boston, MA, May 19–25, 1989.

Additional Resources
Brown C. Computer access in higher education for students with disabilities: a practical guide to the selection and use of adapted computer technology. 2d ed. Sacramento, CA:High-Tech Center for the Disabled, California Community Colleges Chancellor's Office, 1989.

Darling L, ed. Handbook of medical library practice, 4th ed. Vol. I–III. Chicago: Medical Library Association, 1982–88.

Van House NA, et al. Output measures for public libraries: a manual of standardized procedures, 2d ed. Chicago:American Library Association, 1987.

Appendix:
DIRECTORY OF PRODUCTS, PUBLICATIONS, AND ORGANIZATIONS

This listing provides directory information about products, publications, and organizations mentioned as examples throughout the book. It is not intended to be a directory of all computer resources that is useful apart from the book. Inclusion in this listing does not imply endorsement by the authors. Additional sources for specific chapters are listed at the end of the appropriate chapter.

AACR2 (Anglo-American Cataloguing Rules. 2d ed.) (see American Library Association)

Academic Courseware Exchange
  Intellimation
  130 Cremona Drive
  P.O. Box 1922
  Santa Barbara, CA 93116
  (800) 346-8355

American Academy of Otolaryngology
  1101 Vermont Avenue, NW, Suite 302
  Washington, DC 20005
  (202) 289-4607

American Library Association
  50 East Huron Street
  Chicago, IL 60611
  (312) 944-6780; (800) 545-2433
    AACR2 (Anglo-American Cataloguing Rules. 2d ed.)

American Medical Informatics
Association (AAMSI, ACMI, SCAMC)
  1101 Connecticut Avenue, NW, Suite 700
  Washington, DC 20036
  (202) 857-1189

Apple Computer, Inc.
  20525 Mariani Avenue
  Cupertino, CA 95014
  (408) 996-1010
    Apple IIe
    AppleShare
    AppleTalk
    Finder
    ImageWriter
    LaserWriter
    LocalTalk
    Macintosh (SE, SE/30, Macintosh II, Macintosh IIx, Macintosh IIci, Macintosh Plus)
    Macintosh FDHD SuperDrive
    ProDOS
    ResEdit
    System Tools

Apple IIe (see Apple Computer)

AppleShare (see Apple Computer)

AppleTalk (see Apple Computer)

Association of Academic Health
Sciences Library Directors
  c/o Ann Fenner
  Texas Medical Center Library
  1133 M. D. Anderson Boulevard
  Houston Academy of Medicine
  Houston, TX 77030
  (713) 797-1230

Association of American Dental
Schools
  1625 Massachusetts Avenue, NW
  Washington, DC 20036
  (202) 667-9433

Association of American Medical
Colleges
  One Dupont Circle, NW
  Washington, DC 20036
  (202) 828-0400

AST Research
  2121 Alton Avenue
  Irvine, CA 92714
  (714) 863-1333

AT (see IBM)

AVLINE (see National Library of
Medicine)

Biosoft
  P.O. Box 580
  Milltown, NJ 08850
  (201) 613-9013

Books in Print (see R.R. Bowker)

Bookshelf (see Microsoft)

Borland International
  1800 Green Hills Road
  P.O. Box 660001
  Scotts Valley, CA 95066-0001
  (408) 438-8400; (800) 543-7543

BYTE
  Byte Publications
  One Phoenix Mill Lane
  Peterborough, NH 03458
  (603) 924-9281

Campus Technology Products
  P.O. Box 2909
  Leesburg, VA 22075
  (703) 777-9110; (800) 543-8188

Canon BJ-130
  Canon USA, Inc.
  One Canon Plaza
  Lake Success, NY 11042
  (516) 488-6700

Carbon Copy
  Meridian Technology, Inc.
  7 Corporate Park, Suite 100
  Irvine, CA 92714
  (714) 261-1199

Cardiac Arrest Simulation Program
  Aspen Publishers, Inc.
  1600 Research Boulevard
  Rockville, MD 20850
  (800) 638-8437

Cardiovascular Systems and Dynamics
  Command Applied Technology
  P.O. Box 511
  Pullman, WA 99163-0511
  (509) 334-6145

CD-ROM Librarian
  Meckler Publishing Corp.
  11 Ferry Lane West
  Westport, CT 06880
  (203) 226-6967

Cdex-Intellisance
  Cdex Corporation
  1885 Lundy Avenue
  San Jose, CA 95131
  (408) 263-0430

Chambers International
  5499 North Federal Highway,
  Suite A
  Boca Raton, FL 33487
  (407) 997-9444

Chariot Software Group
  3659 India Street, Suite 100
  San Diego, CA 92103
  (619) 298-0202; (800) 242-7468

Claris Corporation
  440 Clyde Avenue
  Mountain View, CA 94043
  (415) 960-1500

Compaq
  Compaq Computer Corp.
  20555 FM 149
  Houston, TX 77070
  (713) 370-0670; (800) 231-0900

Compu-Gard, Inc.
Office Security Systems Department
36 Maple Avenue
Seekonick, MA 02771
(508) 761-4520; (800) 333-6810

Computer Database
Information Access Company
362 Lakeside Drive
Foster City, CA 94404
(415) 378-5000

Copy II Mac
Central Point Software
9700 SW Capitol Highway,
Suite 100
Portland, OR 97219
(503) 244-5782

*Cumulated Index to Nursing & Allied
Health Literature*
Cumulated Index to Nursing &
Allied Health Literature
1509 Wilson Terrace
P.O. Box 871
Glendale, CA 91209-0871

Cyberlog
Cardinal Health Systems, Inc.
7562 Market Place Drive
Eden Prairie, MN 55344-3636
(612) 941-5170

*Datapro Directory of Microcomputer
Software*
Datapro Research
1805 Underwood Boulevard
Delran, NJ 08075
(609) 764-0100; (800) 328-2776

DataShow (see Kodak)

DataShow HR (see Kodak)

DataSources (see Ziff-Davis Publishing
Company)

dBASE IV
Ashton-Tate
20101 Hamilton Avenue
Torrance, CA 90502-1319
(213) 329-8000

DeskJet Plus (see Hewlett-Packard)

DeskWriter (see Hewlett-Packard)

Diconix 300, 300W
Eastman Kodak Co.
Personal Printer Products
901 Elm Grove Road
Rochester, NY 14653-6201
(800) 255-3434

DiscoTest (see Scientific American)

DNASIS (see Hitachi America)

Doss Industries
1224 Mariposa
San Francisco, CA 94107
(415) 861-2223

Drug Information Source
American Society of Hospital
Pharmacists
4630 Montgomery Avenue
Bethesda, MD 20814
(301) 657-3000

EDUCOM
1112 16th Street, NW, Suite 600
Washington, DC 20036
(202) 872-4200

Epson
Epson America, Inc.
Computer Products Division
2780 Lomita Boulevard
Torrance, CA 90505
(213) 539-9140; (800) 922-8911
FX
LQ

Exploring the IBM Personal Computer
(see IBM)

Extron RGB 102E Computer Display
Interface
Extron Electronics
13554 Larwin Circle
Santa Fe Springs, CA 90670
(213) 802-8804

Federation of American Societies for
Experimental Biology (FASEB)
  9650 Rockville Pike
  Bethesda, MD 20814
  (301) 530-7000

Finder (see Apple Computer)

FlipTrack Learning Systems
  999 Main Street, Suite 200
  Glen Ellyn, IL 60137
  (708) 790-1117

FMJ Inc.
  P.O. Box 5248
  Torrance, CA 90510
  (213) 632-0751

FX (see Epson)

Global Computer Supplies
  3318 East Del Amo Boulevard,
  Dept. 92
  Compton, CA 90220
  (213) 603-2266; (800) 845-6225

Grateful Med (see National Library of
Medicine)

Hands-off-the-Program
  Systems Consulting, Inc.
  Box 111209
  Pittsburgh, PA 15238-0609
  (412) 963-1624

Hayes
  Hayes Microcomputer Products, Inc.
  P.O. Box 105203
  Atlanta, GA 30348
  (404) 449-8791

HDCopy
  Glenco Engineering, Inc.
  721 West Algonquin Rd.
  Arlington Heights, IL 60005
  (708) 364-7638

Health Sciences Communications
Association
  5105 Lindell Boulevard
  St. Louis, MO 63112
  (314) 725-4722

Health Sciences Consortium
  201 Silver Cedar Court
  Chapel Hill, NC 27514
  (919) 942-8731

Heartlab (see Williams & Wilkins)

Hewlett-Packard
  Hewlett-Packard Co.
  1820 Embarcadero Road
  Palo Alto, CA 94303
  (408) 725-8900; (800) 752-0900
    DeskJet Plus
    DeskWriter
    LaserJet
    ThinkJet

Hitachi America
  Computer Division
  2000 Sierra Point Parkway
  Brisbane, CA 94005-1819
  (415) 589-8300
    DNASIS
    PROSIS

IBM
  International Business Machines
  Corp.
  Old Orchard Road
  Armonk, NY 10504
  (800) 426-2468
    AT
    Exploring the IBM Personal
    Computer
    IBM Graphics
    InfoWindow
    OS/2
    PC
    PC DOS
    ProPrinter
    PS/2 (Models 50, 55sx, 80)
    XT

IBM Academic Computing Conference
  IBM Academic Information Systems
  472 Wheelers Farms Road
  Milford, CT 06460

IBM Graphics (see IBM)

ImageWriter (see Apple Computer)

InfoWindow (see IBM)

InfoWorld
C.W. Communications, Inc.
(subsidiary of Popular Computing,
Inc.)
1060 Marsh Road, Suite C-200
Menlo Park, CA 94025
(415) 328-4602

Inmac
2465 Augustine Drive
P.O. Box 58031
Santa Clara, CA 95054
(individual sales offices in major
metropolitan areas)

*JAMA (Journal of the American Medical
Association)*
American Medical Association
535 North Dearborn Street
Chicago, IL 60610
(312) 645-5000

Kodak
Eastman Kodak Co.
Business Imaging Systems Division
343 State Street, Dept. 412-L
Rochester, NY 14650
(716) 724-4689; (716) 726-2263;
(800) 445-6325, ext. 200A
    DataShow
    DataShow HR
    LC500 projector

LANShell (see LAN Systems)

LANSpool (see LAN Systems)

LAN Systems, Inc. (NY)
599 Broadway, 11th Floor
New York, NY 10012
(212) 431-8484
    LANShell
    LANSpool

The LaserDisk Professional
Pemberton Press, Inc.
11 Tannery Lane
Weston, CT 06883
(800) 248-8466

LaserJet (see Hewlett-Packard)

LaserWriter (see Apple Computer)

LC500 projector (see Kodak)

Lippincott
J.B. Lippincott Co.
East Washington Square
Philadelphia, PA 19106
(215) 238-4443; (800) 523-2945

LocalTalk (see Apple Computer)

Lotus 1-2-3
Lotus Development Corp.
55 Cambridge Parkway
Cambridge, MA 02142
(617) 577-8500; (800) 345-1043

LQ (see Epson)

MacBaby (Fundamentals of Human
Embryology)
Roy Peterson, Ph.D.
Department of Anatomy
Washington University School of
Medicine
660 South Euclid
St. Louis, MO 63110
(314) 362-3597

Macintosh (SE, SE/30, II, IIx, IIci, Plus)
(see Apple Computer)

Macintosh FDHD SuperDrive (see
Apple Computer)

MacPharmacology
Minnesota Medical Edu-Ware, Inc.
2902 East Superior Street
Duluth, MN 55812
(218) 728-2921

MacUser (see Ziff-Davis Publishing
Co.)

MacWorld
PCW Communications, Inc.
502 Second Street, Suite 600
San Francisco, CA 94107
(415) 546-7722

Map Assist
Fresh Technology Group
1478 North Tech Boulevard,
Suite 101
Gilbert, AZ 85234
(602) 497-4200

MD Computing
Springer-Verlag, Journals
175 Fifth Avenue
New York, NY 10010
(212) 460-1500

Medical Informatics Program (see
National Library of Medicine)

Medical Library Association
Six North Michigan Avenue, Suite
300
Chicago, IL 60602
(312) 419-9094

MEDLINE (see National Library of
Medicine)

Merck, Sharp & Dohme
West Point, Pennsylvania 19486
(215) 661-5000

Microcomputer Index
Learned Information, Inc.
143 Old Marlton Pike
Medford, NJ 08055
(609) 654-6266

Microcomputer Software and
Hardware Guide (see R.R. Bowker)

MicroPro
MicroPro International Corp.
33 San Pablo Avenue
San Rafael, CA 94903
(415) 499-1200; (800) 227-5609

Microsearch Database
Information, Inc.
1725 K Street, NW, Suite 1414
Washington, DC 20006
(202) 833-1174

Microsoft
Microsoft Corp.
16011 Northeast 36th Way
P.O. Box 97017
Redmond, WA 98073-9717
(206) 882-8080; (800) 426-9400
Bookshelf
Microsoft Windows
MS-DOS
Word

Microsoft Windows (see Microsoft)

Misco
1 Misco Plaza
Holmdel, NJ 07733
(201) 946-3500; (800) 631-2227

MS-DOS (see Microsoft)

nView 2 + II
nView Corporation
11835 Canon Boulevard
Newport News, VA 23606
(804) 873-1354

National Library of Medicine
8600 Rockville Pike
Bethesda, MD 20894
(301) 496-6308
AVLINE
Grateful Med
Medical Informatics Program
MEDLINE

NetWare (see Novell)

NetWare Access Server (see Novell)

New England Journal of Medicine (NEJM)
Massachusetts Medical Society
1440 Main Street
Waltham, MA 02254
(800) 843-6356

NeXT
NeXT, Inc.
3475 Deer Creek Road
Palo Alto, CA 94304
(415) 424-0200

Novell
  Novell, Inc.
  122 East 1700 South
  Provo, UT 84601
  (801) 379-5900; (800) 453-1267
    NetWare
    NetWare Access Server

OCLC
  Online Computer Library Center,
  Inc.
  6565 Frantz Road
  Dublin, OH 43017
  (614) 764-6000

Online, Inc.
  11 Tannery Lane
  Weston, CT 06883
  (203) 227-8466; (800) 248-8466
    ONLINE Meeting
    SOFT

ONLINE Meeting (see Online, Inc.)

Opti-Net
  Online Products Corp.
  20251 Century Boulevard
  Germantown, MD 20874
  (301) 428-3700; (800) 922-9204

OS/2 (see IBM)

PC (see IBM)

PC Anywhere
  Dynamic Microprocessor Associates
  60 East 42nd Street, Suite 1100
  New York, NY 10165
  (212) 687-7115

PC Chalkboard
  Lan Fan, Inc.
  P.O. Box 357
  Orem, UT 84057
  (801) 226-8916

PC DOS (see IBM)

PC Magazine (see Ziff-Davis Publishing
Co.)

PC Week (see Ziff-Davis Publishing
Co.)

PDQ (Physician Data Query)
  National Cancer Institute
  International Cancer Institute
  Building 82, Room 113
  Bethesda, MD 20892
  (301) 496-7403

PDR on CD-ROM
  Medical Economics Company, Inc.
  680 Kinderkamack Road
  Oradell, NJ 07649
  (201) 262-3030

Personal Computing
  VNU Business Publications, Inc.
  Ten Holland Drive
  Hasbrouck Heights, NJ 07604
  (201) 393-6000

PFS:Write and PFS:Proof
  Software Publishing Corp.
  1901 Landing Drive
  P.O. Box 7210
  Mountain View, CA 94039-7210
  (415) 962-8910

Pioneer LDV 6000 Series videodisc
player
  Pioneer Communications of America
  600 East Crescent Avenue
  Upper Saddle River, NJ 07458
  (201) 327-6400; (800) 527-3766

Power Menu
  Brown Bag Software
  2105 South Bascom, Suite 164
  Campbell, CA 95008
  (408) 559-4545; (800) 523-0764

ProCite
  Personal Bibliographic Software, Inc.
  P.O. Box 4250
  Ann Arbor, MI 48106
  (313) 996-1580

ProComm
  Datastorm Technology, Inc.
  1621 Towne Drive, Suite G
  P.O. Box 1471
  Columbia, MO 65205
  (314) 474-8461

ProDOS (see Apple Computer)

ProPrinter (see IBM)

PROSIS (see Hitachi America)

PS/2 (Models 50, 55sx, 80) (see IBM)

PsycLit
American Psychological Association
1200 17th Street, NW
Washington, DC 20036
(202) 955-7600

ResEdit (see Apple Computer)

RLIN
Research Libraries Group, Inc.
Jordan Quadrangle
Stanford, CA 94305
(415) 328-0920

R. R. Bowker
245 West 17th Street
New York, NY 10011
(212) 645-9700; (800) 521-8110
Books in Print
Microcomputer Software &
Hardware Guide
Ulrich's International Periodical
Directory

RxDx (see Williams & Wilkins)

Saber Menu (see Saber Software)

Saber Meter (see Saber Software)

Saber Software
P.O. Box 9088
Dallas, TX 75209
(800) 902-8086
Saber Menu
Saber Meter

Science Citation Index Compact Disc
Institute for Scientific Information
3501 Market Street
Philadelphia, PA 19104
(215) 386-0100, ext. 1418;
(800) 523-4092

Scientific American, Inc.
415 Madison Avenue
New York, NY 10017
(212) 754-0550
DiscoTest
Scientific American Medicine

Scientific American Medicine (see
Scientific American, Inc.)

Secret Disk II
Lattice, Inc.
2500 South Highland Avenue
Lombard, IL 60148
(708) 916-1600

Smartcom
Smart Communications, Inc.
825 Third Avenue, 30th floor
New York, NY 10022
(212) 486-1894

SOFT (Buyers' Guide to Micro
Software) (see Online, Inc.)

Sony
Sony Communications Products
1600 Queen Anne Road
Park Ridge, NJ 07666
(201) 833-5217; (201) 930-1000
1031Q, 1020Q projectors

The Suicidal Adolescent
National Audiovisual Center
8700 Edgeworth Drive
Capitol Heights, MD 20743-3701
(800) 638-1300

Sydney
International Library Systems
2600 South Granville Street
Vancouver, B.C., Canada V6H 3V3
(604) 734-8882

Synsor
Synsor Corp.
14241 NE 200th Street
Woodinville, WA 98072
(206) 481-6600; (800) 426-0193

System Tools (see Apple Computer)

1031Q, 1020Q Projectors (see Sony)

ThinkJet (see Hewlett-Packard)

Thomas Computer Corporation
5633 West Howard Street
Chicago, IL 60648-4041
(312) 647-0880; (800) 621-3906

3COM+
3COM Corp.
3165 Kifer Road
Santa Clara, CA 95052
(408) 562-6400

3M Tattle Tape
3M Co.
Office Systems Division
3M Center, Building 220-10W-01
St. Paul, MN 55144
(612) 733-1110

TOPS
TOPS (Division of Sun
Microsystems)
950 Marina Village Parkway
Alameda, CA 94501
(415) 769-9669; (800) 445-8677

Ulrich's International Periodical Directory
(see R.R. Bowker)

University of Colorado at Denver,
Biomedical Communications
Campus Box AO66
4200 East Ninth Avenue
Denver, CO 80262

University of Missouri, Kansas City,
School of Medicine
2411 Holmes Street
Kansas City, MO 64108
(816) 276-1891

University of Tennessee Information
Technology in the Health Sciences
Conference
ITHSC Program Committee
BIT Center
University of Tennessee, Memphis
877 Madison Avenue
Memphis, TN 38163

The Upjohn Company
7000 Portage Road
Kalamazoo, MI 49001
(616) 323-4000

Williams & Wilkins
428 East Preston Street
Baltimore, MD 21202
(301) 528-4000; (800) 527-5597
Heartlab
RxDx

Wisc-Ware
Academic Computing Center
University of Wisconsin
210 West Dayton Street
Madison, WI 53706
(608) 262-8167

Word (see Microsoft)

WordPerfect
WordPerfect Corp.
1555 North Technology Way
Orem, UT 84057
(801) 225-5000; (800) 321-4566

WordStar (see MicroPro)

XCP, Inc.
40 Elm Street
Dryden, NY 13053
(607) 844-9143; (800) 647-7020

XT (see IBM)

Ziff-Davis Publishing Company
One Park Avenue
New York, NY 10016
(212) 503-3400
DataSources
MacUser
PC Magazine
PC Week

Glossary

The glossary defines technical terms used in this book; the first occurrence of a term has been italicized within the text to indicate its inclusion in the glossary. It is not meant to be comprehensive; the reader is referred to the many published computer dictionaries now available, including those cited here. Many definitions, adapted or excerpted, are used with permission from these seven published sources:

(B) Dictionary of computer terms, 2d ed. by Douglas Downing and Michael Covington, Copyright © 1989, Barron's Educational Series, Inc., Hauppauge, NY.

(C) Freedman A. The computer glossary: the complete illustrated desk reference, 4th ed. New York:AMACOM, 1989; available from The Computer Language Company, Inc., Point Pleasant, PA.

(D) Dictionary of computers, information processing, and telecommunications, 2d ed. by Jerry M. Rosenberg, Copyright © 1987, John Wiley & Sons, Inc., New York, NY.

(I) IBM Disk Operating System Version 3.30 Reference, © 1987 by International Business Machines Corporation.

(M) Macintosh System Software User's Guide Version 6.0.4. Cupertino, CA: Apple, 1989.

(W) Webster's New World Dictionary of Computer Terms, © 1988. Used by permission of the publisher, Webster's New World/Simon & Schuster, Inc., New York.

(WN) Webster's Ninth New Collegiate Dictionary © 1989 by Merriam-Webster, Inc., publisher of the Merriam-Webster® dictionaries.

Access time: The time a computer takes to locate and transfer data to or from storage (W, p. 2).

Antiglare screen guard: A filter to place over a video display to reduce light reflection.

ARCNET: A local area network developed by Datapoint Corporation that interconnects a wide variety of personal computers and workstations via coaxial cable. Twisted wire pairs and fiber optic versions are also available. It uses the token passing access method and transmits at 2.5 megabits per second. ARCNET is a distributed star topology that interconnects up to 255 computers. Introduced in 1968, ARCNET was the first local area network technology (C, p. 31).

Asynchronous: Refers to processes that are not synchronized. For example, most computer terminals use asynchronous data transmission, in which the terminal or the computer is free to transmit any number of characters at any time (B, pp. 27–28).

ATTRIB command: A DOS command that modifies file attributes for a single file, for selected files in a directory, or for all files in a directory level (I, p. 7-22).

AUTOEXEC: In MS-DOS (PC-DOS), AUTOEXEC.BAT is the name of a file that contains commands to be executed whenever the computer boots up (B, p. 28).

Backup copy: A copy of a file or data set that is kept for reference in case the original file or data set is destroyed (D, p. 44).

BASIC: From Beginner's All-purpose Symbolic Instruction Code; a programming language with a small repertoire of commands and a simple syntax, primarily designed for numerical application (D, p. 48).

BASICA: In PC-DOS (MS-DOS) on the IBM PC family of computers, the command BASICA calls up an interpreter for a special version of Microsoft BASIC. This interpreter uses code stored on a ROM chip inside the computer; it works only on IBM machines (B, p. 37).

BAT file: From BATch file; in Microsoft DOS and OS/2, a set of operating system commands that is executed as if each command were interactively entered one at a time (C, p. 52).

Baud rate: The transmission rate that is, in effect, synonymous with signal events, usually bits per second (D, p. 50).

Bit: From BInary digiT; a single digit in a binary number (1 or 0); groups of bits make up storage units in the computer called characters, bytes, or words, which are manipulated as a group (C, p. 65).

Board: A printed circuit board, sometimes called a *card*. Many computers, such as the IBM-PC, contain expansion slots where you can add additional boards to enhance the capability of the machine (B, p. 52).

Boot: To start a computer up. The term (earlier bootstrap) derives from the idea that the computer has to "pull itself up by the bootstraps," that is, load into memory a small program that enables it to load larger programs (B, p. 53).

Boot ROM chip: A memory chip that automatically attaches to a LAN file server and starts up the LAN software eliminating the need for start-up batch files on a floppy or hard disk. This is a read-only process that cannot be altered.

Buffer: A holding area for data (B, p. 55).

Bulletin board: A computer system that functions as a centralized information source and message switching system for a particular interest group (C, p. 80).

Bus: A common channel, or pathway, between hardware devices either internally between components in a computer or externally between terminals and computers in a communications network. When bus architecture is used in a communications network, all terminals and computers are connected to a common channel that is made of twisted wire pairs, coaxial cable, or optical fibers (C, p. 81).

Cache: A place where data can be stored to avoid having to read the data from a slower device such as a disk. For instance, a disk cache stores copies of frequently used disk sectors in RAM so that they can be read without accessing the disk (B, pp. 57, 59).

CAI: From computer-assisted (or aided) instruction; software designed for educational use including tutorials, quizzes, and simulations. These may require the use of peripherals such as videodisc players or only the computer itself.

Cannibalize: To take salvageable parts from (as a disabled machine) for use in building or repairing another machine (WN, p. 201).

Card: Used in text for *printed circuit board;* a flat board that holds chips and other electronic components. The back side of the printed circuit board is printed with electrically conductive pathways between the components (C, pp. 552–3).

Cartridge: A self-contained, removable storage module (C, p. 93); with reference to printers, may contain ink, toner, or fonts.

CD-ROM: From compact disk read-only memory; refers to the use of compact disks similar to audio compact disks as a computer storage medium (B, p. 61).

Central processing unit (CPU): The computing part of the computer made up of the control unit, which extracts the instructions out of memory and executes them, and the arithmetic/logic unit, which performs calculations and comparisons (C, pp. 161–2).

CGA: From Color/Graphics Adapter; a video display board from IBM that is available as a plug-in board for IBM PC and compatible personal computers which generates low-resolution text and graphics. The first graphics standard for the IBM PC now superseded by the EGA and VGA standards (C, p. 100).

Chip: A miniaturized electronic circuit approximately 1/16 to 1/2 inch square and about 1/30 inch thick that holds from a few dozen to several million electronic components (transistors, resistors, etc.); synonymous with *integrated circuit,* and *microelectronic* (C, p. 106).

CHOOSER (Macintosh): A multipurpose desk accessory that lets the user communicate with devices such as printers (M, p. 127).

Circuit board: A board to which is affixed the circuitry of a microprocessor; synonymous with *card* and *circuit card* (D, p. 95).

Coaxial cable: A connecting cable used extensively in audio, video, and communications applications that has a greater transmission capacity (bandwidth) than standard twisted pair telephone wires. There are many varieties of coaxial cable, but their construction is similar (C, p. 123).

Compact disk: A computer data storage device; a single disk, 4.7 inches in diameter, can hold 550 million bytes or characters, the equivalent of more than 100,000 typewritten pages (D, p. 110).

Compatibility: (1) Refers to the ability of two devices to work together; for example, a particular brand of printer is compatible with a particular computer to which it can be connected. This type of compatibility might be called *hardware compatibility.* (2) The ability of two computers to run the same programs. It is important to keep in mind that there are different degrees of compatibility. Many computers claim to be compatible with the IBM PC, but some IBM PC programs contain hardware-dependent features that will not run correctly on non-IBM computers (B, p. 74).

Computer literacy: Knowledge of and fluency in computer usage and terminology (D, p. 117).

CONFIG.SYS: A file of instructions for Microsoft's DOS and OS/2 operating systems executed when the computer is booted or rebooted that allows the operating system to be customized to the user's environment (C, p. 150).

Connectivity: The capability of equipment or systems to be used together, such as a printer with a computer or the different parts of a LAN with each other.

Coprocessors: Additional processors used to speed up operations by handling some of the workload of the main processor (CPU); for example, a math coprocessor option in a personal computer increases the computational speed of the system (C, p. 157).

CPU: See *Central processing unit.*

Daisy-chain: An arrangement of devices connected in series, or one after the other. Any signals transmitted to the devices go to the first device, from the first to the second, and so on (C, p. 171).

Daisy wheel: A print mechanism used to produce letter quality (like a typewriter) printing. The character images are on the end of spokes of a plastic or metal hub. The wheel is spun around until the required character is under the print hammer. Each daisy wheel contains a particular type of font. Changing fonts requires changing the daisy wheel (C, p. 171).

Desk accessories: Programs that handle appointment calendars, calculations, memos, and simple phone tasks (D, p. 166). In the Macintosh environment, software tools that are always available and perform functions such as finding a file, moving to the control program, or describing the application currently in use.

Desktop: Refers to an on-screen representation of a user's desktop in icon/mouse-oriented operating environments (C, p. 205).

Directory: An area of a disk where the names and locations of files are stored (B, p. 102).

Disk drive: a device that enables a computer to read and write data on disks (B, p. 105).

DOS: From Disk Operating System; a program that controls the computer's transfer of data to and from a hard or floppy disk (D, pp. 186–7).

Dot-matrix printer: A printer that forms images out of dots. The common desktop dot-matrix printer that is connected to a personal computer uses one or two columns of dot hammers that are moved serially across the paper. The more dot hammers used, the higher the resolution of the printed image. Twenty-four-pin dot-matrix printers can produce typewriter-like output (C, p. 230).

Driver: A program routine that contains the machine codes necessary to control the operation of a peripheral device (C, p. 235).

EGA: From Enhanced Graphics Adapter; a video display board from IBM that is available as a plug-in board for IBM PC and compatible personal computers. It generates medium-resolution color text and graphics (C, pp. 247–8).

Electronic mail (E-mail): The transmission of letters, messages, and memos over a communications network (C, p. 252).

Emulation: One machine emulates another if it achieves the same results as the machine being emulated. For example, VT-100 emulation means making a computer act exactly like a VT-100 terminal. Emulation is different from simulation, which involves imitating the internal processes, not just the results, of the thing being simulated (B, p. 115).

Ethernet: A type of local area network, originally developed by Xerox Corporation, in which communication takes place by means of radio frequency signals carried by a coaxial cable. On the physical level, there are three types of Ethernet connections: thin-wire Ethernet uses RG-58 coaxial cable, conventional baseband Ethernet uses a thicker cable about 3/8 inch in diameter, and broadband Ethernet modulates the whole Ethernet signal on a higher-frequency carrier so that several signals can be carried simultaneously on a single cable, as is the case with TV channels (B, p. 118).

External: See *Internal/external.*

File: (1) In data management, refers to a collection of related records; (2) in word processing, refers to a single text document; (3) in computer graphics, refers to a set of image descriptors for one picture, either in television-like format (raster graphics) or in line format (vector graphics); (4) in programming, the source program and machine language program are stored as individual files; (5) in computer operations, refers to any collection of data that is treated as a single unit on a peripheral device, such as all of the examples in items 1 through 4 above (C, p. 280).

File server: A computer on a local area network that stores the programs and data files shared by the users connected to the network and acts like a remote disk drive to the users in the network. Also called a *network server* (C, p. 282).

Finder, MultiFinder: Components of the Macintosh's operating system that manage the desktop by keeping track of all the icons on the desktop and controlling the Clipboard and Scrapbook. They also let you copy files from one disk to another. Finder is the single tasking version, and MultiFinder is the multitasking version (C, p. 283).

Floppy disk: A removable storage medium used with many varieties of computers and word processing systems; a single round disk of flexible, tape-like material that is housed in a square envelope or cartridge. Like magnetic tape, floppy disks can be recorded, erased, and used over and over again (C, p. 287).

FORTRAN: From FORmula TRANslator; developed in 1954 by IBM, the first high-level programming language and compiler developed for computers. It was originally designed to express mathematical formulas, and although it is used occasionally for business applications, it is still the most widely used language for scientific, engineering, and mathematical problems (C, p. 295).

Giga: A prefix for billion abbreviated as *G* (C, p. 310).

Graphics: With regard to the computer, the creation and processing of picture images (C, p. 313).

Hard disk: A data-recording system using solid disks of magnetic material turning at high speed (D, p. 266).

HD (high density): The provision of a high storage capacity per unit storage space, for example, in bits per inch (D, p. 271).

Hypermedia: Refers to the use of data, text, graphics, video, and voice as elements in a Hypertext system. All the various forms of information are linked together so that a user can easily move from one to another (C, p. 340).

IBM-compatible pc (PC compatibility): The original IBM Personal Computer (PC) was designed quickly by IBM and used little new technology; hence, few patents protect it, and it is easy for other companies to make compatible machines (B, pp. 236–7).

Icon: A picture on a computer screen that represents a particular object or command. For example, on a Macintosh computer, the picture of a trash can stands for "delete"; use the mouse to move a file to the trash can, and the file will be deleted (B, p. 160).

Incompatible: Not compatible; see *Compatibility*.

Inkjet printer: A non-impact printer that forms characters by the projection of a jet of ink onto paper (D, p. 292).

Interface: A connection between two devices. Hardware interfaces are the plugs, sockets, and wires that carry electrical signals in a prescribed order. Software interfaces are the languages, codes, and messages that programs use to communicate with each other, such as between an application program and the operating system. User interfaces are the keyboards, mice, joy sticks, light pens, tablets, dialogues, command languages, menus, and display screens used for interactive communication between the user and the computer (C, p. 370).

Internal/external (to CPU, e.g., peripherals): Refers to the location of a device relative to the microcomputer enclosure. A modem board that is within the microcomputer and has been installed onto a slot in the mother board is an internal device. A modem that is designed for use outside the microcomputer through its attachment to the serial port is an external device.

K: According to the Institute of Electrical and Electronic Engineers, uppercase *K* stands for 1,024, and lowercase *k* stands for 1,000 (C, p. 385).

KV: From *kilovolts*; a measure of static electricity propensity that has been determined by methods designated by the American Association of Textile Chemists and Colorists.

LAN: From *local area network*; a network that connects several machines that are located nearby (in the same room or building), thus allowing them to share files and devices such as printers (B, p. 180).

Laser printer: A printer that uses the electrophotographic method used in copy machines to print a page at a time. A laser is used to "paint" the dots of light onto a photographic drum or belt; the toner is applied to the drum or belt and then transferred onto the paper (C, p. 395).

LCD display: A display using *l*iquid *c*rystal *d*iode technology (D, p. 328).

Lenticular screen: See *Lenticule.*

Lenticule: Any of the tiny corrugations or grooves molded or embossed into the surface of a projection screen (WN, p. 684).

Local area network: See *LAN.*

Mainframe computer: A large computer occupying a specially air-conditioned room and supporting typically 100–500 users at a time. The IBM 370 and IBM 3081 are examples of mainframe computers (B, p. 191).

MB: Megabyte; 1,048,576 bytes (D, p. 373).

Memory chip: A chip that holds programs and data either temporarily or permanently. The major categories of memory chips are RAMs and ROMs (C, p. 447).

Memory-resident: A program that remains in memory after being run so that it can be called up later (B, p. 193).

Menu: A list of choices that appears on the screen while a particular program is being executed. Typing the number or letter that corresponds to a particular command operation causes the command to be executed. The presence of menus in a program makes it easy for people to use the program because they don't need to memorize all the commands. The menu shows all the options (B, p. 193).

MHz: From *megahertz;* one million cycles per second.

Micro channel: The bus in high-end models of IBM's PS/2 personal computer series. It differs from the bus in first-generation XTs and ATs by allowing multiprocessing to take place within the computer, that is, two or more microprocessors can perform data processing activities at the same time (C, p. 451).

Microcomputer: A computer whose CPU consists of a single integrated circuit known as the microprocessor. Ordinarily, a microcomputer is used by only one person at a time (B, p. 195).

Minicomputer: A computer intermediate in size between a mainframe computer and a microcomputer; two examples are the Digital Equipment Corporation VAX and the IBM System/3 (B, p. 198).

Modem: From *MOD*ulator-*DEM*odulator; a device that encodes data for transmission over a particular medium, such as telephone lines, coaxial cables, fiber optics, or microwaves (B, p. 199).

Monitor: A display screen that shows the output of a computer, video cassette recorder, or other video-generating device (C, p. 466).

Monochrome: Single color; refers to monitors that display only one color along with black, such as white on black, black on white, green on black, and amber on black (C, p. 467).

Mother board: A rigid frame to which circuit boards are affixed forming the basis of a microprocessor (D, p. 395).

Mouse: A special computer input device, connected by a wire to the computer. A roller on its underside is designed to roll along the desk top beside a computer. Moving the mouse with one hand causes the cursor to move along the screen in the same direction in which the mouse is being moved (B, pp. 204–5).

Mouse pad: A mat used with mouse devices that provides a better surface of contact compared to a tabletop.

MS-DOS: From *MicroSoft Disk Operating System*; an operating system for computers that use the 8086 or 8088 microprocessor. MS-DOS is marketed by IBM as PC-DOS for the IBM PC (B, p. 205).

Network: In communications, the communication path between terminals and computers (C, p. 480).

Network board: A printed circuit board that is installed in a microcomputer and has the network wiring attached to it enabling the microcomputer to communicate with other network components, such as the file server.

Node: An individual computer (or occasionally another type of machine) in a network (B, p. 212).

Operating system: A master control program that runs the computer and acts as a scheduler and traffic cop. It is the first program loaded (copied) into the computer's memory after the computer is turned on; the central core, or kernel, of the operating system must reside in memory at all times (C, p. 496).

Optical scanner: An input device that reads into the computer characters and images that are printed or painted on a paper form (C, p. 500).

OS/2: An operating system that was developed by Microsoft for the IBM PC AT and PS/2 computers that runs only on machines with 80286 or 80386 microprocessors. OS/2 is a multitasking operating system; that is, it enables the computer to shift its attention rapidly back and forth between several processes, seemingly running several programs at the same time (B, p. 222).

Parabolic lighting: Light fixture arrangements that bend light to provide an even illumination.

Parallel port: An external interface to a printer or other peripheral device (C, p. 514).

Pascal: A programming language, developed by Niklaus Wirth, designed to encourage programmers to write modular and well-structured programs (B, p. 232).

PC-DOS: Another term for Microsoft's DOS operating system that runs on IBM personal computers. The term is often used to differentiate between the DOS operating system supplied with an IBM machine and the MS-DOS version supplied with an IBM compatible machine. PC-DOS and MS-DOS are usually identical except for the way they deal with the BASIC programming language. IBM compatible computers are often tested with PC-DOS to find out how compatible they truly are (C, p. 521).

Peer-to-peer communications: The communicating from one user to another user in the network. It implies the ability to initiate the session at the user's discretion (C, p. 523).

Peripheral: Any hardware device connected to a computer, such as monitors, keyboards, printers, plotters, disk and tape drives, graphics tablets, scanners, joy sticks, game paddles, and mice (C, p. 523).

Port: A connection between the CPU and another device that provides a means for information to enter or leave the computer (B, p. 243).

PostScript: A page description language from Adobe Corporation that was initially used in Apple's LaserWriter laser printer and is now supported by many other printer manufacturers. It provides a language that an application program can use to describe text fonts and graphics images for printing and requires a PostScript printer and a word processing, desktop publishing, or other program that generates printer output in PostScript format. PostScript printers have built-in CPUs and memory and perform the graphics and font creation internally (C, p. 549).

Printout: In computer technology, the printed output of a computer (D, p. 480).

Processor: See *Central processing unit.*

ProDOS: From *PRO*fessional *D*isk *O*perating *S*ystem; an Apple II operating system designed to support mass storage devices and floppy disk storage devices.

Productivity software: Computer programs that assist people in performing specific tasks, such as word processing or spreadsheet development.

Public domain software: Software not copyrighted, and freely exchanged and copied (D, p. 497).

RAM: From *R*andom-*A*ccess *M*emory; a memory device whereby any location in memory can be found, on average, as quickly as any other location. A computer's RAM is its main memory where it can store data, so the size of the RAM (measured in kilobytes) is an important indicator of the capacity of the computer (B, p. 261).

RAM-resident programs: Multitasking programs making it possible to run several different programs at the same time, allowing one to switch effortlessly back and forth between a spreadsheet, database, word-processing program, and the like, transferring data between these applications as needed. Once loaded they remain in the computer's memory and can be called up at any time by means of a couple of keystrokes (D, p. 509).

RENAME command: A DOS command that changes the name of the file specified in the first parameter to the name and extension given in the second parameter (I, p. 7-183).

RGB monitor: A color monitor that uses separate signals for the three additive primary colors (red, green, and blue). Each primary color is either on or off at any moment; for example, yellow is displayed by turning red and green on and blue off. Only eight colors can be displayed using this system (B, p. 272).

ROM: From Read-Only Memory; contains computer instructions that do not need to be changed, such as the instructions for calculating arithmetic functions. The computer can read instructions out of ROM, but no data can be stored in ROM (B, p. 273).

Root directory: The main directory of a disk, containing files and/or subdirectories (B, p. 273).

SCSI port ("scuzzy"): From Small Computer Systems Interface (SCSI); a standard bus for connecting devices such as disk drives to computers that is different from the internal bus by which the CPU communicates with memory (B, p. 279).

Self-boot: A system or software that has the capability of starting up on its own through instructions of an AUTOEXEC file without additional action by the user other than turning on the microcomputer.

Serial port: An I/O port through which data is transmitted and received serially; used for communicating with terminals (D, p. 567), and serial peripheral devices such as modems, videodisc players, and some printers.

Server: A machine on a network that provides a particular service to other machines; for instance, a disk server manages a large disk, and a print server manages a printer (B, p. 282).

Shareware: Software that is copyrighted but can be distributed free of charge to anyone. Users are asked or required to make a payment directly to the author if they use the program regularly (B, p. 283).

Slot: A socket in a microcomputer designed to accept a plug-in circuit board (B, p. 287).

Software: The set of programs that tell the computer what to do. The term software is contrasted with hardware, which refers to the actual physical machines that make up a computer system (B, p. 288).

Spooling: From simultaneous peripheral operations on line; with personal computers, it refers to printing a document or file in the background while allowing the user to work on something else (C, p. 646).

Spreadsheet: a software program that simulates a paper spreadsheet, or worksheet, in which columns of numbers are summed for budgets and plans (C, p. 646).

Stand-alone: Descriptive of a single, self-contained computer system, as opposed to a terminal that is connected to and dependent upon a remote computer system. A stand-alone device will operate by itself, requiring no other equipment (W, p. 358).

Star network: A communications network in which all the terminals are connected to a central computer. Local area networks, such as IBM's Token Ring and AT&T's Starlan are examples of a star network (C, p. 662).

Subdirectory: A disk directory that is stored in another directory (B, p. 295).

Surge protector: A unit that plugs into a wall socket to protect computers from alternating current line surges (D, p. 617).

Switch box: A device for channeling communication among more than one terminal, printer, etc.; for example, one printer can be used by two computers with the use of a switch box.

System folder: In the Macintosh environment, includes the main components of the Macintosh operating system: finder, system, printer drivers, and multifinder.

System tools (Macintosh): Utility programs in the Macintosh environment, including activities such as repairing disks and moving desk accessories.

Telecommunications: The transfer of data from one place to another over communications lines (W, p. 376).

Timesharing: A way of running more than one program on the same computer at the same time so that, for example, the computer can serve many users at different terminals simultaneously (B, p. 303).

Token ring network: (1) A communications network that uses the token passing technology in a sequential manner. Each station in the network passes the token on to the station next to it. (2) A local area network developed by IBM that interconnects personal computers via a special cable containing twisted wire pairs. It uses the token passing access method and transmits at four megabits per second. Token Ring uses a star topology, in which all computers connect to a central wiring hub, but passes tokens to each of up to 255 stations in a sequential, ring-like sequence (C, pp. 696–7).

Topology: The physical or logical placement of nodes in a computer network (D, p. 654).

Trash (Macintosh): Receptacle for items to be thrown away such as documents, folders, applications (M, p. 111).

Twisted pair: A pair of small insulated wires that are commonly used in telephone cables. The wires are twisted around each other to minimize interference from other wires in the cable. Cables containing from one to several hundred twisted pairs are used in myriads of electronic and telephone interconnections. Such wires have limited bandwidths compared to coaxial cable or optical fiber (C, p. 713).

UCSD p-System: From University of California at San Diego p-System; a software development system designed for transportability across different computers. Programs written in this system can run on several computers without change. The programs are written in traditional languages, such as BASIC and Pascal, but UCSD p-System compilers are used to translate the language into an interim language called p-code. The p-code is executed by an interpreter program in the target machine (C, p. 715).

Uninterruptible power supply: A power supply that uses batteries to continue providing electricity to a computer for a few minutes in the event of a power failure making it possible to shut down the computer in an orderly way without losing data (B, p. 316).

Vaccine: A computer program that offers protection from viruses by making additional checks of the integrity of the operating system. No vaccine can offer complete protection against all viruses (B, p. 320).

Version: A separate program product, based on an existing program product, that usually has significant new code or new function. Each version has its own license, terms, conditions, product type number, monthly charge, documentation, test allowance (if applicable), and programming support category (D, p. 688).

VGA: From *Video Graphics Array;* A display system that is built into various models of the PS/2, IBM's second generation personal computer series. VGA boards are also available on boards for plugging into first generation IBM compatible pcs. VGA supports previous IBM display standards; thus software written for MDA, CGA, and EGA display modes will also run under VGA (C, p. 731).

Videodisc (or videodisk): A record-like device storing a large amount of audio and visual information that can be linked to a computer; one side can store the pictures and sounds for 54,000 separate TV screens (D, p. 690).

Virus: A program that is used to infect the operation of a computer system. After the virus code is written, it is buried within an existing program, and, once that program is loaded into the computer, the virus replicates by attaching copies of itself to other programs in the system (C, p. 737).

White board: A white, erasable surface on which various colors of felt-tip markers can be used for writing.

Wide area network: A set of widely separated computers connected together; for example, the worldwide airline reservation system is a wide area network (B, p. 327).

Word processing: The management of text documents that replaces all the operations normally associated with a typewriter (C, p. 754).

Workstation: A configuration of computer equipment designed for use by one person at a time. This may have a terminal connected to a computer, or it may be a stand-alone system with local processing capability. Examples of workstations are a stand-alone graphics system and a word processor (W, p. 409).

Index